Parenting

FROM SURVIVING
TO THRIVING

D1057543

Parenting

FROM SURVIVING
TO THRIVING

BUILDING STRONG FAMILIES

IN A CHANGING WORLD

CHARLES R. SWINDOLL

THOMAS NELSON
Since 1798

NASHVILLE   DALLAS   MEXICO CITY   RIO DE JANEIRO   BEIJING

Published in Nashville, Tennessee, by Thomas Nelson. Thomas Nelson is a registered trademark of Thomas Nelson, Inc.

Thomas Nelson, Inc. titles may be purchased in bulk for educational, business, fund-raising, or sales promotional use. For information, please e-mail SpecialMarkets@ThomasNelson.com.

All Scripture quotations, unless otherwise indicated, are taken from New American Standard Bible. © 1960, 1962, 1963, 1968, 1971, 1973, 1975, 1977, 1995 by The Lockman Foundation, La Habra, California. Used by permission.

Other Scripture references are from the following sources:

> *The Message* (MSG), © by Eugene H. Peterson, 1993, 1994, 1995, 1996. Used by permission of NavPress Publishing Group.

> The NET Bible® (NET) © 2003 by Biblical Studies Press, L.L.C. www.netbible.com All rights reserved. Used by permission.

> THE AMPLIFIED BIBLE (AMP), Old Testament © 1965, 1987 by the Zondervan Corporation. The Amplified New Testament © 1958, 1987 by the Lockman Foundation. Used by permission.

> The *Holy Bible*, New Living Translation (NLT), © 1996. Used by permission of Tyndale House Publishers, Inc., Wheaton, Illinois 60189. All rights reserved.

Editorial Staff: Shady Oaks Studio, 1507 Shirley Way, Bedford, TX 76022.
Cover Design: TOBIAS' OUTERWEAR FOR BOOKS
Page Design: Inside Out Design & Typesetting, Fort Worth, TX

Published in association with Yates & Yates, www.yates2.com.

Library of Congress Cataloging-in-Publication Data

Swindoll, Charles R.
   Parenting—from surviving to thriving : building strong families in a changing world / by Charles R. Swindoll.
      p. cm.
   Summary: "Practical and inspiring ways to parenting that not only thrive but survive the tests of time"—Provided by publisher.
   Includes bibliographical references and index.

   ISBN 978-1-4002-8003-2 (trade paper)
   1. Parenting—Religious aspects—Christianity. 2. Parents—Religious life. I. Title.
BV4529.S95   2006
248.8'45—dc22   9184   2006029971

Printed in the United States of America
08 09 10 11 12   RRD   9 8 7 6 5 4 3 2 1

It is with great delight that I dedicate this volume
to all ten of our grandchildren:

Ryan, Chelsea, and Landon Swindoll

Parker and Heather Nelson

Ashley, Austin, and Jonathan Dane

Noah and Jessica Swindoll

These wonderful children, these fine young men and
women, represent the delicious fruit of our family tree.
Their lives will enrich and enhance their generation,
thanks to the great training they have received.
Cynthia and I adore each one
with all our hearts.

Contents

Contents

Introduction

Several years ago, I read an article in the *Los Angeles Times* containing a letter to the advice columnist Ann Landers, and to this day it still haunts me. A mother wrote the letter at age seventy, having reared five children. In response to the question, "Was it worth it?" she responded:

> No. The early years were difficult. Illness, rebellion, lack of motivation (we called it shiftlessness and laziness in our day).
>
> One was seriously disturbed—in and out of mental hospitals. Another went the Gay Lib route. Two are now living in communes (we never hear from them). Another has gone loony with the help of a phony religious leader who should be in jail.
>
> Not one of our children has given us any pleasure. God knows we did our best, but we were failures as parents and they are failures as people.

She signed it, "Sad Story."[1]

Introduction

This is a woman living every parent's nightmare. When we bring that little bundle home from the hospital and recover from the shock of being completely responsible for the care and well-being of another person, an alien thought takes up residence in the back of our minds: *What if I fail as a parent?* Take it from a parent of four and a grandparent of ten . . . as you grow older, you discover the futility of trying to overpower that nagging fear, and after a few failures, you learn to embrace it. After all, failure is inevitable. As someone wisely wrote, "Guilt is an occupational hazard of parenting."

Fortunately, failure on the level of "Sad Story's" is very rare and extremely remote. In fact, I am convinced that much of the heartache we accept as a normal part of childrearing is avoidable. The "terrible twos" can actually have their fun moments given a good sense of humor. The onset of puberty, with its turbulent, hormone-driven angst, can provide the perfect opportunity to strengthen the bond between parent and child. And I reject the notion that the teenage years must necessarily involve rebellion and conflict.

I don't suggest that the years will be free of heartache, pain, confusion, conflict, or even periods of rebellion and estrangement if we apply principles from God's Word. However, those trials don't have to characterize and overshadow the entire child-rearing process. This I offer as hope from one coming to the topic of parenting from several angles: five, to be exact. In addition to my approach as a student of God's Word, I write as a realist, as a son, as a parent, and as a grandparent.

AS A REALIST . . .

I understand that tips and so-called keys to parenting rarely work out as easily as many would like you to think. So I want you to know that any application of a principle from Scripture will be offered with that in mind. While I believe these principles to be sound and they are proven to be effective by the experience of a number of people, you will have to use discernment. You must evaluate your own unique set of challenges and adjust the applications to fit. And always keep in mind: no principle is airtight.

I also understand that not everyone reading this book is a new parent. To those who have been rearing children for several years now, some of this information will cause you frustration and guilt. There's no such thing as a perfect parent, so without a doubt you have failed pretty badly in some areas. Obviously—and sadly—we cannot undo past mistakes. I confess that I would give just about anything for another chance to apply the principles I discovered only after the blunders. But we can spend the rest of our years languishing in the backwash of bad memories, or face forward and resolve to create a more positive future. Let's choose the latter. While we cannot correct past mistakes, we can repair and rebuild. I have found over a lot of parenting years that it's never too late to begin the healing process.

AS A SON . . .

I will be very transparent about my own upbringing, although I want to be careful in how I do that. I don't want you to misjudge my mother and father. Just like you, I was not reared perfectly. My parents made some mistakes with me. Some affected me so deeply that I determined to discover a better way from the Scriptures. But I'll quickly and very honestly say that my parents were also some of the finest people I have ever known! If everyone had parents like mine, not only would families be in better shape, but the world would be a much better place.

As a Parent . . .

I remember the evening after Cynthia gave birth to our first child. As soon as I got back from the hospital, I dropped to my knees in our tiny, three-room campus apartment and I cried out to God, "Please help me know how to be a dad. Cynthia's never been a mom. We don't know what we're doing, so dear Father, please help us!" We dove into the Scriptures, and the Lord began to reveal some of the things I'll be sharing in the chapters to come. God answered my prayer by providing direction through His Word. He rescued our children from some of the worst mistakes we could have made, and where we applied those principles, our children thrived.

Just as my parents made mistakes with me, Cynthia and I have made mistakes with our children. I will be candid where appropriate and share with you the lessons I learned and what I would have done differently, looking back. My hope is that you will avoid making those same mistakes yourself or, if you have already made them, you will be encouraged. Just as Cynthia and I were able to bring healing to those wounds with our children, so you can with yours.

As a Grandparent . . .

As a father of four adult children—each with families of his or her own—I can look back on a history of successes and mistakes. And as I think of each of our ten grandchildren, I am further convinced that each boy and girl is valuable and worth my time. I didn't know what it was like to have a father spend much personal time with me, so I had to cultivate what didn't come naturally. As a grandfather, I know now more than ever that each child takes time and attention to discover—*lots* of time and *lots* of attention. They can benefit from all you can give them. I only wish I had known that better when my children were small.

Fortunately, from my position as a grandfather, I can see how my children have built upon the parenting they received to become even better moms and dads. And from this vantage point, I can assure you that your failures will not doom your children to a horrible future. God's grace superabounds where sin abounds. Your love will cover a multitude of mistakes. This overwhelming responsibility is not so overwhelming when you recognize that your children really belong to the Lord, and He will not fail you if you diligently and sincerely seek Him.

And as an Author . . .

I am extremely grateful for my friends at Thomas Nelson, especially Mike Hyatt and David Moberg. Their support, encouragement, and confidence fuel my fire. And I must add here how much fun it is to work on another book with my son-in-law,

Mark Gaither, as my editor and with Mary Hollingsworth and her splendid team at Shady Oaks Studio in Fort Worth. Without their combined efforts, these pages would be hard to endure—*for you and me*!

Finally, my greatest thanks to Cynthia, since she's been through all these parenting years with me . . . never giving up, never losing hope, and never walking out.

—CHUCK SWINDOLL
Frisco, Texas

ONE

The Best-Kept Secret of Wise Parenting

good place to start is for me to give you a little background information.

My mom and dad married on October 5, 1930. The following August 5, 1931, my brother Orville was born. (If you do the math, it adds up right, so I'm not revealing any scandal here.) Then on September 8, 1932, they welcomed my sister and named her Lucille after my mother. Most everyone today knows her as Luci. A couple of years later, on October 18, 1934, I came along. I was, in my mother's words, "a mistake." My parents didn't resent my arrival, but bringing me into the world was certainly not something they had planned, and I was never quite able to forget that. Orville was clearly my mother's favored child, Luci was undoubtedly my father's favorite, which left me wondering where I fit in.

Both Orville and Luci had a lot of impressive qualities, so they deserved all of the attention and praise they received. My brother is brilliant. I don't know whether he ever took an IQ test, but he would no doubt score in the "approaching genius" category. He was also greatly gifted as a musician. I'm convinced he could have been a concert pianist if had chosen that as a career. But the heart of this talented genius lay elsewhere. He attended Rice Institute, now called Rice University, and ultimately wound up serving the Lord full time as a missionary in Buenos Aires for more than thirty years.

Luci is among the most gifted people I have ever known. As most of you would agree, she is absolutely contagious in her enthusiasm and has a voracious appetite for living. She sang for many years with the Dallas Civic Opera and brings an amazing artistic flair to everything she does—the rooms of her lovely home, right down to the pages of her personal journals, would be worth photographing. Being a fine author, she has written several excellent volumes. Many of you know of her books and her ministry with Women of Faith.

So with a brother and sister like that, you can imagine how comparisons might be potentially damaging to a younger sibling. Take school for example. Orville's report cards were downright boring! Absolutely predictable. All one letter—A. Mine? Now mine had variety. I was all over the board, spanning the full gamut of scores. But my parents didn't seem to appreciate this broad variety in my education. I know because they frequently compared me to my brother as they routinely suggested that I should "work hard to be more like him." I instinctively knew that I was a unique individual with different interests and gifts, but I seldom felt that those differences were acknowledged or appreciated. Comparisons can be stinging. They were regular reminders that I was not like him, which caused me to resent and feel inadequate around my brother. To this day, Orville and I aren't close. But I have to admit, much of that is my problem. I'm not sure I would know how to be.

Please don't think that I had an unhappy childhood or was reared in a terrible family. I was reasonably happy in my home, sometimes deliriously happy and carefree. We were a loving family who often laughed and sang together. I can still remember standing between my brother and sister on the marble drugstore counter at the local pharmacy in El Campo, Texas, during World War II, singing at the top of our lungs, "Heil (phttt!), heil (phttt!) right in the Fuhrer's face!" (They just don't write 'em like they used to!) We each received a double-dip ice-cream cone for our performances.

Our house was always filled with music, especially during the Christmas season. My brother accompanied on piano with my dad on the harmonica while my sister and I sang. My mother had been a soprano soloist before starting a family and had a very accomplished singing voice. This winsome, musical family of mine sparked my interest in the arts, not only classical music, but great literature, especially poetry, and the theater. To this day I am fascinated by all the performing arts.

So, on the whole, I had a healthy, happy childhood. Nevertheless, every home has its challenges, and this happened to be mine: I never felt wanted or respected by either of my parents . . . not deeply. I can't remember many times when I was affirmed by them. And I honestly don't think that they ever really knew who I was, which left them ill equipped to help me know myself.

That, by the way, is a primary responsibility of parenting. Put succinctly, a parent's job is to know his or her child and then help that child discover who that unique, precious person is before God and in the world around him or her. When that objective is accomplished and the time comes to release that life to live independently, the child can leave with a strong sense of identity, which will provide both security and direction for the rest of life.

The best-kept secret of wise parenting, therefore, is this:

THE JOB OF A PARENT IS TO HELP HIS OR HER CHILDREN
COME TO KNOW THEMSELVES, GROW TO LIKE THEMSELVES,
AND FIND SATISFACTION IN BEING THEMSELVES.

My parents taught me obedience, discipline, compassion, generosity, responsibility, and most important of all, how to have a relationship with Jesus Christ. Godliness was the single most important standard in our home. But for all the good training I received from my mom and dad, I started life somewhat on my own without a clue as to who I was. They didn't know me, so how could they have shown me?

LEARNING TO ADAPT

Many years later, Cynthia and I were living in Dallas while I attended Dallas Theological Seminary. I was in my third year of that four-year degree program, taking twenty-one hours and auditing two other courses, including one I called Rabid Greek Reading with Dr. Stan Toussaint. (The course syllabus called it

4

Rapid Greek Reading, but I knew better.) Another in that scholarly mix of classes was one taught by my wonderful mentor, Dr. Howard Hendricks called The Christian Home. That course of study changed everything for me.

I was especially motivated to learn because in September of that year we had brought home from the hospital our firstborn, a little boy we named Curt. I earnestly prayed for help from the Lord because I felt completely unprepared to be a father. I desperately wanted to avoid the mistakes my parents had made with me. This class was a major part of God's answer. And because I wasn't sure where to start with my study in Scripture, I turned to Proverbs, thinking that if any book in the Bible could provide wisdom it would be that one. About that same time, I became serious about studying the Hebrew text and benefited from the superb skills of Dr. Bruce Waltke, whom I deeply admire for his profound knowledge of the Semitic languages.

My study took me several years. I learned childrearing principles from Scripture, applied them, failed, analyzed my mistakes, adjusted, and tried again. Then, during the time I served as the pastor of a church in Irving, Texas, a suburb of Dallas, I would visit Dr. Waltke to have him critique my understanding of the Hebrew verses I was studying. I began to develop parenting principles from some key verses in the Old Testament that I found insightful. I wanted to be certain my interpretation was accurate, especially since it was so different from how I had heard them explained before.

Our job as students of the Bible is not to dream up new interpretations and innovative theology, but to discover the original meanings and uncover theology that has been twisted and obscured over time. I became convinced that the "standard" interpretations of some important passages on childrearing were tragically flawed and were being taught to others. So I was careful to have a respected theologian and Hebrew scholar help to keep me honest.

If you'll allow me to fast-forward from my childhood and young adulthood to today, I'd like to reveal what I discovered and what my wife and I put into practice with our own children.

PROVERBS 22:6 . . . THE RIGHT WAY

Train up a child in the way he should go,
Even when he is old he will not depart from it.

This verse in most biblical childrearing manuals has a standard interpretation that goes something like this:

"Rear your children as moral, upright, God-fearing, churchgoing kids. Be sure they carry a Bible to church, attend lots of Sunday school classes, and each summer attend Christian camps. Enforce your rules and regulations with consistency and discipline. Make sure they learn the Ten Commandments, the Golden Rule, and several key verses of Scripture. Teach them to pray, and be sure they come to a saving knowledge of Jesus Christ. After all, they're eventually going to sow their wild oats as they are certain to rebel. They'll live in that rebellious lifestyle for a while, then, once their oats are sown and they tire of their fling with the wild side of life—

when they're old and decrepit—they'll come back to the Lord . . . but only if you raised them right!"

I don't know about you, but I don't find that very comforting. Frankly, that is not much of a promise. Yet for some reason it has become "the Christian method of childrearing." Why anyone would take comfort in that is beyond me. It doesn't sound like something God would hold out to us, saying, "This is wise counsel. Do this and everything will turn out well!"

Not only is that popular interpretation of Proverbs 22:6 not very comforting, but *it isn't true*! You and I know people who were reared like that, who ran wild and never came back. They grew up with Christian parents in a moral, consistent, strict home only to run wild when they graduated and then *died* in their rebellion. And they never did stop departing from "the way he should go."

If we dig beneath the surface and go back to the Hebrew language to discover what the human writer, under the direction of the Holy Spirit, intended to say, we'll find something very different than what we've been taught. What we have in this verse is a very refreshing, common-sense approach to childrearing that offers hope, yes, but more importantly, practical guidance. Realistic direction is what I have come to expect from Scripture, and I'm never disappointed.

Hebrew is a language of artists and poets. Almost every word has a metaphorical connection to something in the experience of these people. Hebrew poetry, especially, uses allusion and word pictures that convey meaning by analogy, so that a rich tableau of cultural associations stands behind even the simplest sentences. English has some of these, but not nearly as many, or to the degree, as Hebrew.

Proverbs 22:6 drips with poetic allusion and metaphor. And it is typical of Hebrew poetry in that it is very concise—only eight words. Because each word packs so much cultural meaning, drawing so heavily on word pictures, we'll carefully observe each one.

"Train up"

"Train up" comes from the Hebrew verb *hanakh*, which means "to dedicate, or consecrate."[1] It's used only four times in the Old Testament—three in reference to dedicating a building, and here of a child. Interestingly, the noun form of this verb means "mouth." In similar Semitic languages, such as Aramaic and Arabic, the term means "palate, roof of mouth, jaws, lower part of mouth, lower jaw of horse, mouth, etc."[2] Knowing how this word fit the ancient, Near Eastern culture will help us understand the term as it is being used here.

The Arabic verb, a very close cousin to this Hebrew word, is a term used to describe the custom of a midwife, who dipped her index finger into a pool of crushed dates or grapes in order to massage the palate of a newborn's mouth. This trained—or rather, encouraged—the baby's sucking instinct so that nursing came more easily. And in keeping with the "mouth" idea, the term in Arabic also means "make experienced, submissive, etc. (as one does a horse by a rope in its mouth)."[3]

So in the term *hanakh* we have the mingled ideas of "dedicate," "train," "mouth," "make experienced," and from the horse's bridle allusion, a sense of subduing for the purpose of teaching and guiding. These multiple allusions to culture have been the subject of controversy for expositors, some of whom want to narrow the meaning to a single definition. This might be a reasonable approach if this weren't poetry. As one Hebrew scholar put it,

> Poetic segmentation, or regulation, characteristically depends upon brevity of expression. To that end, poetry employs abundant imagery and figures of speech. Such terseness sometimes heightens ambiguity, or rather, increases the possibility of multiple meanings.[4]

Put simply, poetry has the power to convey several, very complex ideas all at once so that the meaning is multilayered and profound. Hold on to these ideas as we fit the term *hanakh* into the rest of the line.

"a child"

The Hebrew word translated "child" is intriguing. The translation leads us to believe that the verse has a little boy or girl in mind. But the Hebrew term *na'ar* is much broader. It is used to refer to young people in all stages of growth. In 1 Samuel 4:21, *na'ar* is a newborn. In Exodus 2:6, Moses is a three-month-old *na'ar*; and in 1 Samuel 1:22, Samuel, the *na'ar*, has yet to be weaned. First Samuel 3:1 uses the term to describe Samuel as a young lad serving Eli in the temple. *Na'ar* in Genesis 21:12

pictures Ishmael as a preteen, while in Genesis 37:2, Joseph is a seventeen-year-old *na'ar*. The young men who served as David's messengers in 1 Samuel 25:5 are called *na'ar*, as was a young man of marriageable age in Genesis 34:19.

While *na'ar* can be a little child, it can also be a young man or woman of any age still living under a parent's roof or in the care of an authority figure. Keep that in mind as we continue unraveling the verse.

"the way he should go"

The clear meaning of the verse turns on the phrase "in the way he should go." Parents commonly think there is but one way a child should go: *their way*. They may think the way they were reared was and still is the right way, or they may think some method they find in a psychologist's manual or a book by a famous theologian or pastor is "the way." They read the phrase "the way he *should* go," and they assume that is "the way." *Wrong.*

The literal Hebrew is "in accordance with his way," or even more literally, "upon the mouth of his way." (There's "mouth" again, forming a wordplay with *hanakh*.) Some scholars say that the book of Proverbs presents only two "ways" a person can go: the way of the righteous wise or the way of the sinful fool.[5] In a broad sense, that's right. But the brilliant and very complex use of words in this poetic Hebrew expression suggests that this advice goes far beyond the obvious.

The key word in this phrase is *derek*, which means "way" or "road." It can even mean "characteristic manner," as in Proverbs 30:18–19:

There are three things which are too wonderful for me,
Four which I do not understand:
The *way* of an eagle in the sky,
The *way* of a serpent on a rock,
The *way* of a ship in the middle of the sea,
And the *way* of a man with a maid. (emphasis added)

In keeping with the poetic spirit of this proverb, both meanings are likely with an emphasis on the characteristic manner of the child.

We receive our children from the hand of God, not as soft, pliable lumps of clay, ready to be molded into what *we* think they should become. Each child comes with a set of abilities, intellectual capacity, and a way of perceiving and thinking, all of which were endowed by God. We can surely influence and even mold them to a certain extent, but our efforts have limits. On the one hand, if parents ignore or discourage a talent, it may never emerge. On the other hand, if parents cultivate a talent, it will likely become a part of the child. (Please pause and read this paragraph again, only more slowly.)

So, then, putting it all together, we have a verse that says, "Dedicate, inaugurate, induce, make experienced and submissive the one you call 'son' or 'daughter' according to his or her way defined by each child's characteristic manner."

Children are as unique as snowflakes. Even within the same family, two boys born of the same mother and father and reared in the same environment can be completely different. One is strong and determined, while another is meek and easily persuaded. One is organized; the other is messy and unorganized. One is academically gifted; the other excels in sports, art, or mechanics. One might be a natural-born leader, while the other prefers to follow and to serve others in a supportive role. Some kids are generally optimistic and upbeat, while others are more naturally melancholy and dreamy.

Parents usually make the mistake of trying to rear all their children using identical methods. "This is the way my dad did it. That's the way I'm gonna do it." His methods may have been acceptable . . . for rearing you! But that was you. Your child isn't you! Your child has different parents, with a different mix of genes and interests and influences than yours. You can use family traits to gain insight, but even that must be a part of the observation process because each child is different.

Think about some of the better-known figures of the Bible. Adam and Eve gave birth to Cain and Abel, who could not have been more different young men. Remember the twins Jacob and Esau? How different were they? Esau was an outdoorsman, a rough-and-ready hunter, while Jacob was more cultured and refined, preferring the comforts of home and fixing meals in the kitchen. Jesse's oldest son, Eliab, when compared to his youngest, David: nothing alike. Eliab didn't write psalms. Eliab was deceiving and jealous while David proved to be heroic, unselfish, humble, creative, and independent. Same parents. Same household. Completely different men.

I am convinced that one major reason for rebellion among young men and women is that they have expectations put upon them that are unsuited for their "way." Parents will hold out one child as a model for the others to imitate—a futile expectation given what we know about each child's uniqueness. Or a parent may have a particular dream that he or she expects the child to fulfill. I know a dad who paid his son to play football despite the son's obvious artistic interests. Why? Because the dad was never able to realize his own dream due to limitations in his own life. So he wants to see his son have the dream he couldn't. That's understandable from a certain point of view. But it's terribly frustrating and can be downright destructive. Young people want to discover themselves and find their own ways, not have someone else's ideas of who they are and what they should be forced on them.

How then do we know the "way" our child should take? By observing his or her "way." Proverbs 20:11–12 says, "Even a young man is known by his actions, whether his activity is pure and whether it is right. The ear that hears and the eye that sees—the Lord has made them both" (NET).

Your children are making themselves known every day. Don't drift. Don't let your senses get dull. Don't ignore what you're hearing and seeing. Pay attention to your children while they are at play. Carefully observe what they do, how they do things, and what they enjoy. Those are eloquent clues, frequently repeated. So pay attention! When you see your children do things well, encourage and affirm them. If children clearly enjoy particular kinds of activities, provide more opportunity to explore them. And as children experiment, give them plenty of room to fail and try something else without a single word of condemnation and without calling attention to the mess or criticizing the expense.

"when he is old"

The word translated "old" in this picturesque language is derived from the image of hair on the chin. In other words, the young person should be well on his or her journey to adulthood by the time the first physical signs of maturity begin to appear—not when he or she has one foot in the grave after a lifetime of rebellion. Boys begin to grow their first whiskers—tender as those wisps of beard may be—between the ages of fifteen and seventeen. So we would expect the age for young women to correspond.

"will not depart from it"

The Hebrew verb is simply "turn aside." What a great graduation gift! Imagine the sense of accomplishment and hope and eagerness in the hearts of high school graduates who have healthy self-awareness and clearly identifiable paths to walk. Imagine all the angst and rebellion that they would bypass. So many only begin to grope their way to the right path after graduation, sometimes wandering through the dark valleys of booze, drugs, immoral and/or illegal behavior, and dysfunctional romances. Or they might suffer several career false starts . . . or even broken marriages.

Help your children know themselves, like themselves, and be themselves, and their paths will become self-evident. Their paths will be a natural fit to the people they grow up to become. Why, then, should they want to turn away from that? This is not only good for helping children vocationally. The same principle applies to children's spiritual development.

Here is my paraphrase of this proverb with all the above in mind: "Cultivate a thirst, initiate a hunger, create an appetite for spiritual things in the lives of children of any age, as long as they are living under your roof, and do it in keeping with the way they are bent—disciplining the disobedience and the evil while affirming and encouraging the good, the artistic, the beautiful. As children begin to grow into adults, their paths will be aimed directly toward the Savior, and they will continue to walk in His sovereignty."

A PRINCIPLE VERSUS A PROMISE

Many people mistake proverbs for airtight promises. The verse seems to have the Lord saying, "If you do X, I will see to it that Y is always the result." Unfortunately, childrearing is not an exact science, and sometimes the math doesn't balance out. God does make promises in the Bible, and He keeps them. A proverb, however, is a principle for living. As long as we live in a world filled with sin, our best efforts will sometimes be met with failure.

Children have wills of their own, which means that, unlike machines, you can do everything correctly and not have the result you hoped for. You can prepare your children to make wise, responsible decisions; nevertheless, the choices remain theirs. And as unfair as this is, the consequences will be theirs . . . *and* yours. Even when we have them store their harvest of wild oats in their own barns, we as parents will pay a heavy emotional toll.

15

If you have an older child who is living in rebellion or who has chosen a life contrary to the one you prepared for him or her, I encourage you to drop at least one burden: *self-blame*. Any parent can say without hesitation that he or she could have done better. All parents with grown children have things that make us cringe when we look back on our previous performance. Naturally, the failures come to mind first. And perhaps you have, indeed, done a very poor job as a father or mother. Maybe you struggled with issues that kept you from being the parent you otherwise could have been. Nevertheless, the choices were your child's to make. In a later chapter, we'll address the topics of reconciliation and restoration. For now, focus on what you can do in the present to be the very best parent possible.

An Observation Observed

I want to close this chapter with a real-life example of how to observe a child by using a typical outing with my granddaughter Jessica. Jessica is a little red-haired pistol who will one day rule the world (if she has her way about it). She's only in the third grade, so we can't say for sure who she will be and what she is best suited to do with her life upon graduation from high school. Predicting the future is not the point of observing. This is only one snapshot to be followed by a thousand more between now and then. And all along the way, we'll be reflecting the best of what we see in her so that she will come to know herself, like herself, and be herself.

A couple of years ago Cynthia wanted to do some shopping at the local mall to purchase some things for an upcoming trip, and Jess happened to be staying with us that weekend. When I told her the plans, mentioning that the three of us would be going to the store that evening, she said, "Now, Bubba, I have to have all my papers."

"Papers?"

"Yes, I need three sheets of paper and a pen. You need to get me a pen."

So within a few moments I found myself running errands for a first grader. I grabbed a pen and a few sheets of paper, which she wanted cut into smaller sheets. She placed them in the big slicer we have in my home office, and I was sure she was going to lose a thumb, so I reached over to help. She gave me a serious look and said, "I *know* how to run this."

"Oh, okay. I didn't realize."

Before long, she was buckled into the seat of my pickup truck, and the three of us were headed to the mall. In her hands she had a pen and three sheets of paper—all different sizes. When we hit Nordstrom, Cynthia's favorite department store, Jess and I found a couple of comfortable seats provided for weary husbands (thank goodness for those), and I learned that we were not there to relax. Absolutely not! We were to write down everything we did. Everything.

Sat down.
Saw clothes.
Did cartwheels.
Tried to keep Bubba awake.

After a little while of this, I said, "You know what, Jess? You're exhausting me."

She said, "Bubba, we're on a mission!" She then added, "We're now going to write down everything we *see*."

Lights.
Dresses.
Floor.
Bench.
Old man.
Salesperson.

She kept at it the whole trip and had me working with her. Here I am, twice her size and more than sixty years older, but I'm following her around! Could there be the stirrings of leadership in this little girl? What might her attention to detail say about her? And her complete lack of concern for the sheets of paper cut to different sizes? These could mean nothing, but over time, they may help us—all of the adults in her life—learn who Jess is becoming so that we can show her.

After the trip, I wrote a note to my son and my daughter-in-law telling them what a delightful child Jessica is, what a great job they are doing as parents, and that I see in her evidence of good health, protection, care, determination, and love. She is learning to know who she is, like who she is, and be who she is. She is well on her way to becoming the person God made her to be.

Jessica will need plenty of direction and correction along

the way. (Count on it!) She will need constant encouragement and occasional rebuke. She will need lots and lots of time from the adults in her life and, most especially, from her parents. They will need to keep her a very high priority in their lives.

I recently read the following true story about evangelist Billy Graham:

His fame was growing rapidly, beginning fifty years ago during a spectacular series of meetings held in Los Angeles. Thousands of people were coming—including film stars and athletes and all kinds of celebrities. They all came to hear the man, to meet with the man. As the series entered its eighth week in L.A., it was consuming all of Graham's time and energy. God was speaking through him in powerful ways.

Toward the end of the crusade, Graham's sister-in-law and her husband came to Los Angeles, bringing a baby with them.

The evangelist squeezed in time to be with his relatives. During that meeting he made a comment that the little girl was cute; he asked, "To whom does she belong?"

The sister-in-law's mouth dropped open in surprise. "Why? She's yours. She's yours, Billy."

Mr. Graham had been away from home so long he didn't even recognize his own little Anne when she was brought to the crusade. That night the great evangelist resolved that he would spend more time at home with his children.[6]

Don't be fooled by the "quality time" myth. *Quantity* time is what will be required of you as a parent—your primary role in life over the next several years. It takes time to know someone else deeply. Lots of time. Time you don't think you have but must find. Time to stop, look, listen, encourage, and love. Time, looking back, you'll never regret.

TWO

Understanding How Your Child Was Made

*J*ust about the time I feel like an expert on childrearing, I get a big dose of reality. During the 1970s, Cynthia and I had four small children, and we stayed busy applying the principles we learned from Scripture with some measure of success. During that time, I traveled to Venezuela to minister to a wonderful, very responsive group of men and women serving as missionaries. Most of them had families. Feeling a little more like an expert than I was, I chose to speak on how to rear children. I felt pretty good about the talks I gave. Throughout the week, nobody threw anything at me—in fact, they seemed to appreciate what I presented. After delivering my last message and saying good-bye, I boarded a 747 for home. Once I had settled into my seat, I looked back on those days and thought, *Not bad, Swindoll*! I had no idea that I would soon be brought back to reality.

As I savored the success, I was also pleased to notice that the middle seat next to me was empty—the only unoccupied seat on the entire plane. And I thought, *Thank You, Lord. It's a reward, I realize, and I'm very grateful.* Then, just before the main door swung closed, a little Venezuelan woman boarded the plane—with twins. I earnestly prayed that I had over-looked a row of empty seats *far* to the rear of the plane, but no. The middle was her seat . . . or I should say *their* seat.

I didn't know any Spanish, but apparently my face or my smile indicated to her that I would help, so she quickly handed me one of the twins. By the way, the one she chose to hold was asleep, but not mine. The twin I held never slept. I tried every-thing I knew to keep that kid happy and quiet, but he was a mixture of Curious George, Hercules, and the Road Runner. While his mother and sister slept peacefully beside me, he screamed and kicked and vomited and pooped and belched and squirmed and fought nonstop. Everything finally came to a grand climax when the flight attendants served the meal.

Back in those days, they served soup as a part of dinner and . . . BOOM! One good kick and I was wearing it. Right then, I realized that childrearing looks easy on paper and sounds fairly simple from the pulpit. But there are times . . . oh, you can finish the sentence. So as I've matured as a pastor and seen my children through every stage, let me assure you that I am the furthest thing from a childrearing expert. I can easily identify with the experience of author Charlie Shedd:

All over the midwest I gave [the same speech]. They paid me a handsome fee and they were glad to get me. "This guy will wow you." That's what they said, and the people came. With high hopes they came for "How to Raise Your Children."

Then we had a child! . . .

Those brilliant ideas had such a droll sound at 2:00 a.m. with the baby in full cry!

In my defense I want you to know this—I kept on trying. I changed my title to "Some Suggestions to Parents," and charged bravely on. Then we had two more children and altered it again. This time it came out "Feeble Hints to Fellow-Strugglers." . . .

So today I seldom speak on parenthood. And whenever I do, after one or two old jokes, you'd catch this uncertain sound, "Anyone here got a few words of wisdom?"[1]

That's how I feel anytime I approach the subject of child-rearing. Fortunately, I don't have to be an expert. I have at my disposal a Book of wisdom that provides the direction we need to invest the very best in our children. As a seasoned father and grandfather, I can offer a few tidbits that will be helpful, but my desire is to open the Scriptures to you as plainly as possible and then suggest some ways to apply the principles we find. So let's go there together.

THREE UNCHANGING TRUTHS TO ACKNOWLEDGE

Childrearing methods come and go faster than fad diets, but God's Word remains immutable. We can rely on His unchanging truths. Three of them will help you understand how your child was made, which is the first step to applying childrearing tools with wisdom. Keeping these truths in mind will make observing your child's behavior more insightful and your guidance more productive.

A Bent Child Will Stay "Bent" Without Parental Guidance

My using the word "bent" when referring to a child sometimes raises a few eyebrows. I get the word from a key image in Proverbs 22:6. We covered this verse very carefully in the previous chapter. I wrote about the Hebrew word *derek*, which means "way," "road," or "characteristic manner." One visual image associated with *derek* is that of an archer's bow, which has a natural curvature to it. Psalm 7:12 uses the verb form of this root word to picture the Lord as having "bent His bow and made it ready." An archer in ancient days would put his foot on the curved piece of wood and bend the bow in order to string it.

Each child, like a bow, comes with a shape, or a bent, that is natural to him or her. If a bow is to be useful, it cannot remain in its natural, relaxed state. An archer must work with the bow's characteristic curvature, so he can bend the wood in the right direction, and string it so that it might become a source of power. Obviously, an unstrung bow cannot launch arrows.

Proverbs 29:15 says, "The rod and reproof give wisdom, but a child who gets his own way brings shame to his mother." The literal Hebrew behind this proverb is complicated, so translators do their best to supply a meaningful interpretation. In this case, I prefer rendering it faithfully and preserving the difficulty. The latter half of the proverb reads, literally, "but a child left brings shame to his mother."

"A child left" doesn't mean left out in the cold or abandoned. The most likely meaning is "left in the condition in which he was born." It's an unusual form of the Hebrew verb that could also be translated "let go" or even "sent away." A child having certain gifts and bents who is delivered into the hands of parents and who is left without instruction, training, boundaries, discipline, and direction will ultimately shame them. The picture is one of neglect, lack of concern, or passivity on the part of the parent, resulting in a child out of control.

Take note of the tools used to guide a child: "the rod and reproof." (We'll go into more detail on this in a later chapter.) Some expositors say that the Hebrew should be rendered "a reproving rod" or "a rod of reproof," but I think Solomon had two distinct ideas in mind: the rod, a physical instrument of discipline; and reproof, verbal correction. A wise parent employs both in order to keep rebellious disobedience in a child from becoming full-blown temper tantrums and wild displays of rage.

Of course, "the rod" is a visual image of corporal punishment, but it's not limited to that. The bigger idea is that of consequences. For younger children, this could be a spanking or a meaningful time-out. For older kids, it could be grounding, removing privileges, or restricting the use of property. The point of "the rod," in whatever form it takes, is to get the message across: "Your actions will have repercussions." Spanking is one form of "the rod," but it's not the only one.

"Reproof" is verbal correction, which must *always* accompany punishment. Every use of the rod also requires instruction, an explanation of what went wrong and why the rod was necessary, an affirmation of the child's value, and a reminder of how much he or she is loved. All of this must be done in private. Never, ever discipline a child in public or in front of the family. Nothing is gained by embarrassing the child. In fact, the humiliation will likely drown any constructive message he or she might otherwise hear.

Perhaps the most difficult part of the discipline process is maintaining the proper balance between the rod and reproof. Each child responds differently to each. Some young children can't hear without a proper spanking (again, I will describe corporal punishment in detail in the next chapter); others hardly require any spankings at all. And for some, punishment of any kind shuts down communication and actually encourages rebellion. Then to make the balance even more challenging, as the child ages, he or she needs less rod and more reproof.

Each Child Is Bent Toward Evil

Foolishness is bound up in the heart of a child; the rod of discipline will remove it far from him. (Proverbs 22:15)

We use the word *foolishness* too lightly in our culture. "Oh, cut out that foolishness" or, "Kids today are full of foolishness," almost as if foolishness is nothing more than childlike mischievousness. However, in the Old Testament, "foolishness" is a severe term. The Hebrew term translated "foolishness" means "a state of being devoid of wisdom and understanding, with a focus on the evil behaviors which occur in this state."[2] It is the word used to describe the mind-set and behavior of a morally corrupt individual who lives his or her life in rebellion to God. So this is no trivial word. Furthermore, the Bible says that every child is born with this bent toward evil. He inherited it from his parents, and they from theirs. Tracing it back to its original source, the entire human race received it from our common ancestor, Adam.

This evil bent is what the New Testament calls "the flesh." Theologians often call it "the sin nature." You will notice that a child doesn't have to be taught how to disobey, to lie, or to behave selfishly. This comes as naturally to a toddler as sleeping because it is "bound up in the heart."

In the Near Eastern culture and language, the heart is not merely the organ that pumps blood. The heart is a symbolic term for the inner being, the mind, the thought processes, the volition, the emotions, the inner life of the person. Authors Harris, Archer, and Waltke describe the term this way:

In its abstract meanings, "heart" became the richest biblical term for the totality of man's inner or immaterial nature. In biblical literature it is the most frequently used term for man's immaterial personality functions as well as the most inclusive term for them since, in the Bible, virtually every immaterial function of man is attributed to the "heart." . . .

The heart is the seat of the will. A decision may be described as "setting" the heart (2 Chronicles 12:14). "Not of

my heart" expresses "not of my will" (Numbers 16:28). . . .
Closely connected to the preceding is the heart as the seat of
moral responsibility. Righteousness is "integrity of heart"
(Genesis 20:5). Moral reformation is to set one's "heart right"
(Job 11:13). The heart is described as the seat of moral evil
(Jeremiah 17:9).[3]

According to Psalm 51, this corruption of the heart begins
not with birth, but is a part of our nature rooted in the moment
of conception. "Behold, I was brought forth in iniquity, and in
sin my mother conceived me" (Psalm 51:5).

David uses the very strong word "iniquity," which means
wickedness, wrongdoing, or something worthy of punishment. The
Hebrew verb means "to bend, twist, distort."[4] This is a synonym for
perversity—something grotesquely contorted out of its original
shape. And he goes on to say, "In sin my mother conceived me."

Now, this statement can be easily misunderstood. The NET
Bible offers a very helpful explanation:

The psalmist is not suggesting that he was conceived
through an inappropriate sexual relationship (although the
verse has sometimes been understood to mean that, or even
that *all* sexual relationships are sinful). The psalmist's point
is that he has been a sinner from the very moment his
personal existence began. By going back beyond the time of
birth to the moment of conception, the psalmist makes his
point more emphatically in the second line than in the
first.[5]

The Amplified Bible reads, "Behold, I was brought forth in [a state of] iniquity; my mother was sinful who conceived me [and I too am sinful]."

As dear and loving and caring and sacrificial as our mothers and fathers may have been, a depraved, sinful nature characterized them . . . and they, in turn, passed it on to us just like DNA at conception. Then, when we are born as tiny babies, we're already at odds with God, possessing an inborn bent to reject His way for our own. And the only remedy is the miraculous transformation accomplished by Jesus Christ when we believe in Him.

Parental instruction leads to this crucial decision, but it cannot replace it. The rod and reproof can—and must—guide the child toward this saving knowledge, and they can provide the child with the necessary skills to function normally in society, but they can do nothing to cure the heart of the deadly, inherited disease called "sin."

David, in another psalm, says, "The wicked are estranged from the womb; these who speak lies go astray from birth" (Psalm 58:3). Isaiah 48:8 adds, "You have been called a rebel from birth." And these are only a small sampling of verses that speak to the bent of all people toward evil as a part of our nature from conception and birth.

The evil bent in a child is undeniable. If left alone, it will drive him to do almost anything to have his own way. James Dobson tells a story of a ten-year-old terror who perfectly illustrated the principle, "A child left brings shame to his mother."

[Robert] was a patient of my good friend Dr. William Slonecker. Dr. Slonecker and his pediatric staff dreaded the days when Robert was scheduled for an office visit. He literally attacked the clinic, grabbing instruments and files and telephones. His passive mother could do little more than shake her head in bewilderment.

During one physical examination, Dr. Slonecker observed severe cavities in Robert's teeth and knew that the boy must be referred to a local dentist. But who would be given the honor? A referral like Robert could mean the end of a professional friendship. Dr. Slonecker eventually decided to send him to an older dentist who reportedly understood children. The confrontation that followed now stands as one of the classic moments in the history of human conflict.

Robert arrived in the dental office, prepared for battle.

"Get in the chair, young man," said the doctor.

"No chance!" replied the boy.

"Son, I told you to climb onto the chair, and that's what I intend for you to do," said the dentist.

Robert stared at his opponent for a moment and then replied, "If you make me get in that chair, I will take off all my clothes."

The dentist calmly said, "Son, take 'em off."

The boy forthwith removed his shirt, undershirt, shoes and socks, and then looked up in defiance.

"All right, son," said the dentist, "now get on the chair."

"You didn't hear me," sputtered Robert. "I said if you make me get on the chair, I'll take off all my clothes."

"Son, take 'em off," replied the man.

Robert proceeded to remove his pants and shorts, and finally stood totally naked before the dentist and his assistant.

"Now, son, get in the chair," said the doctor.

Robert did as he was told and sat cooperatively through the entire procedure. When the cavities were drilled and filled, he was instructed to step down from the chair.

"Give me my clothes now," said the boy.

"I'm sorry," replied the dentist. "Tell your mother that we're going keep your clothes tonight. She can pick them up tomorrow."

Can you comprehend the shock Robert's mother received when the door to the waiting room opened and there stood her pink son, as naked as the day he was born? The room was filled with patients, but Robert and his mom walked past them and into the hall. They went down a public elevator and into the parking lot, ignoring the snickers of onlookers.

The next day, Robert's mother returned to retrieve his clothes and asked to have a word with the dentist. However, she did not come to protest. These were her sentiments: "You don't know how much I appreciate what happened here yesterday. You see, Robert has been black-mailing me about his clothes for years. Whenever we are in a public place, such as a grocery store, he makes unreasonable demands of me. If I don't immediately buy him what he wants, he threatens to take off all his clothes. You are the first person who has called his bluff, Doctor, and the impact on Robert has been incredible!"[6]

Beating in the chest of every child is a strong, selfish will like Robert's. Not many have Robert's daring, but they all have that potential. He wanted to be happy and thought that by having his own way, he could avoid painful experiences, like having a tooth drilled, and could sate his impulses, like eating treats from the grocery store line. He obviously didn't know what was best for him, yet he knew no other alternative. He had no boundaries upon which to rely.

Children crave well-defined, unmovable boundaries to help them make sense of the world around them. No child wants to be his or her own authority. It's frightening. It causes him or her to grow increasingly insecure, fearful, defiant, and willful. But disciplining a child requires consistent self-discipline by the parent. Defining and enforcing healthy boundaries for a child is the most difficult part of being a mom or dad. No one wants to be the heavy.

Let's face it, we'd rather have our child's love and hugs than to have him or her view us as the enemy—even for a short time. But if we're willing to be the "bad guy" in order to give our child's world order and definition, the result will be a home free of chaos, where everyone can enjoy freedom and love, acceptance and security, purpose, direction, and an authentic basis for a strong self-image. Curb the evil bent with consistent, reasonable consequences and you will create more opportunity to engage your child's more pleasant side. And you'll also find yourself receiving far more love and hugs from a child who looks to you for order and security.

Each Child Was Created by God with a Bent Toward Good

Now, the good news is that childrearing involves more than hammering away at a child's evil bent. In fact, depending upon the child, the majority of your time and energy should go into developing the wondrous amount of good that God created in him or her.

Psalm 139 is a prayer that celebrates the image of God in people and praises our Creator for His amazing care and awareness: "O LORD, You have searched me and known me. You know when I sit down and when I rise up; you understand my thought from afar" (Psalm 139:1–2).

This doesn't portray God sitting light-years off in a distant heaven, looking down on a speck named Chuck wandering around on planet Earth. "Understanding my thought from afar" means that He knows my thoughts long before I have them. He knows what I'm going to say and what I'm going to do before either happens, not only because He knows the future, but because He knows *me*. He knows me intimately. The same is true of you. You are more than a nameless dot amongst six billion other dots. He knows you individually.

"You scrutinize my path and my lying down, and are intimately acquainted with all my ways" (Psalm 139:3).

The Hebrew word for "scrutinize" is the same word for "winnow": to spread out, to scatter for the purpose of examination. Picture the Lord pouring out our deeds onto a table like puzzle pieces and sifting through the pile, examining each piece. That's the idea behind this term. And the word "you" in this verse is emphatic. *You* sift through my behavior. He has taken personal responsibility to know us individually.

He scrutinizes our "path and lying down," our manner of living, and He is completely familiar with our *derek*. We discovered that *derek* means "way," "road," or "characteristic manner." In this verse, *derek* is plural. In other words, He knows all our deeds, how we do them, and why—all of our choices, all of our mannerisms, all of our abilities, all of our limitations, everything that contributes to who we are as individuals. How is this possible?

"For You formed my inward parts; you wove me in my mother's womb" (Psalm 139:13).

The term translated "inward parts" is the word for kidneys, which the psalmist uses both literally and figuratively. Literally, kidneys represented the sum total of a person's internal organs. "When used figuratively, the term refers to the innermost aspects of personality."[7] These the Lord "wove" together. Think of the planning and care that must go into the weaving of a lovely tapestry. Each thread, each color, chosen with a particular end in mind and carefully interlaced to make something both useful and beautiful.

The Lord fashioned each child with meticulous care for nine months in his or her mother's womb. Long before Mom and Dad ever feel the skin of their baby or look on his or her face, the Lord wove together a unique set of mannerisms, gifts, interests, intellectual abilities, emotions, skills, attitudes, and He interconnected them with bone, blood, muscle, nerves, and a brain. And to think that some regard this work of divine art—a certified original—as little more than unwanted fetal tissue to be flushed down a toilet.

After considering all of these details, David reached a climax in verse 14 with a burst of praise:

"I will give thanks to You, for I am fearfully and wonderfully made; wonderful are Your works, and my soul knows it very well" (Psalm 139:14).

In verse 15, David turned to the physical aspect of his being.

"My frame was not hidden from You, when I was made in secret, and skillfully wrought in the depths of the earth" (Psalm 139:15).

Everything has a frame, a structure that gives it a particular size and shape. God gave us a skeleton, prescribing the density, the thickness, and the length of each bone. And putting those together gives us the height He intended us to have, which is a significant point for the junior high kid who stands 6'8" . . . as a girl. Suddenly the fact that God designed her body and made her unique in that way becomes extremely important. She needs to know all that!

We can say with confidence to our children, "You're tall

because God wanted you to be tall." Or, "You're small or stocky or thin or redheaded because the Lord designed you to be that way. Thank God you're not just like everyone else!" He gave some children a bright, bubbly personality and others He made more melancholy. Some He made multitalented, while others have a singular, outstanding gift. And because He made each one specifically to order, we can treasure each one as a unique gift.

Each person He "skillfully wrought in the depths of the earth." To the Jew, "the depths of the earth" was a deep, mysterious, unknowable place having sacred significance. David uses this expression to refer to the mother's womb, where, in secret, the Lord meticulously designed and fashioned the body and personality that the child should have.

"Your eyes have seen my unformed substance; and in Your book were all written the days that were ordained for me, when as yet there was not one of them" (Psalm 139:16).

This has God's sovereignty written all through it. The Lord saw a design before there was substance. In some situations, this particular verb, translated "to see," means "take delight in, take pleasure." I can picture God looking into a mother's womb, rubbing His hands together with eager anticipation—yet another opportunity to fashion another work of art. As He thinks of what He will create, a smile forms on His lips, along with the words, "Yes, that's just right, just the way I want it."

When we look upon a toddler, what do we typically see? Spit-up, grass stains, untied shoelaces, a bundle of needs, and constant demands. What if, instead, we asked, "What remarkable person will this one become?" "What gifts and abilities will emerge soon?" "How will this one fit into God's grand design for the world?"

I look back on my own experience, and I wonder how my life would have been different if my parents had taken the time to know me and then communicated what they saw back to me. I was an adult in the Marine Corps, for example, before I ever knew that I possessed leadership skills. A wise parent will take time to understand how God made his or her child and then work with His design to let it flourish early:

"You know, honey, we notice that when your friends come over for a party, you take charge. That shows me that you have a knack for leadership that we need to develop."

"You have such an analytical mind. You're quick to pick up some of these things. That's terrific. Let's see what we can do with this mind of yours."

"You love to listen to music, don't you? What instrument do you like to hear the most? Let's try out some private lessons."

Imagine how this approach would affect a child's thinking about himself and the future. Imagine what a healthy sense of security the child would have in knowing herself, accepting herself, and learning to be herself. Imagine how much more immune to negative peer pressure and ridicule a child would be, knowing that God's design was unfolding within him or her and that you were there to help him or her see it. This is an extension of the primary point in the previous chapter:

THE JOB OF A PARENT IS TO HELP HIS OR HER CHILDREN
COME TO KNOW THEMSELVES, GROW TO LIKE THEMSELVES,
AND FIND SATISFACTION IN BEING THEMSELVES.

Apllying the Knowledge of How Your Child Was Made

Using discipline, "the rod and reproof," to correct the bent toward evil and guide the child toward a personal relationship with Jesus Christ is a necessary part of parenting. Dealing with rebellious, defiant behavior requires discipline on the part of the parent because no one likes being the "bad guy" to a child. But if it's done correctly, the discipline process actually creates more opportunity to bond with him or her and to focus on the aspect of parenting we find more enjoyable.

Then, just as the Lord knows each of His children intimately, we must seek to know our child well. That requires time, keen observation, patience, interaction, and lots of prayer. But if we put effort into this crucial responsibility as a parent, our children will reap benefits long after they have become adults. I can name at least three.

First, *every adult longs to have memories of a parent's love.* I have found some measure of healing in my own life by giving my own children what I desired so much from my parents. It's an odd kind of melancholy relief that I find soothing. Whatever else I may have done poorly, I know that my children know that I love them.

Second, *every adult wants to have a strong sense of personal control*—control of life circumstances, control over self during temptation, control over choices that affect the future. I took no command of my life when I graduated from high school. I merely followed in the steps that seemed to come next. I had no particular passion, no specific pursuit. Fortunately, the Lord took control of my life through a series of circumstances that made little sense until many years later. How much better for a child to know who he or she is, the Lord's plans for the world, and how he or she will serve Him. That knowledge gives an adult the tools necessary to make wise, responsible, God-honoring decisions.

Third, *every adult desires to feel the security of self-respect.* When a growing child understands how God put him or her together, when adulthood comes, he or she enjoys well-defined personal boundaries. These boundaries provide a person the strength to stand his or her ground in the face of injustice, abuse, or attempted manipulation. Because others have little room to toy with his or her identity, he or she is virtually immune to exploitation. This, by the way, includes Satan's attacks as well. A strong sense of identity in Christ is the best defense against the devil's chief weapon: deception.

Action Steps Worth Taking

Now let me turn these into actions we can apply.

First, *determine to know your child's uniqueness.* Knowledge of your child will not come to you automatically. This will require keen observation and sensitive determination to seek the knowledge you need. Turn each day with your child into an opportunity to discover who he or she is on the inside. I'm not suggesting you watch and record their actions like they're a bunch of lab rats. Learn to know them like you would any other person—a friend, a mate. Spend lots of time with them that has no agenda. Communicate. Ask questions. Observe what makes your child happy, bored, stimulated, agitated, angry. Look for natural gifts in athletics, music, and academics. Talk to teachers, youth leaders, and other parents. Be deliberate about discovering each child's identity.

As you do this, you will cultivate a deepening love for your child. You cannot love someone you don't know, but knowing him or her allows greater opportunity to feel and show love. The child, in return, will gain self-awareness, the first step to self-discipline.

Second, *discipline yourself to set limits on your child's will.* This is hard work and it's unpleasant. Standing around a dental office looking bewildered won't do anything to help a boy like Robert. But curbing his willful defiance at age ten will help you gain enough control over his behavior to help him control himself by the time he reaches older adolescence. This doesn't mean that children will never disobey or push against your boundaries, but it will keep chaos from ruling the home and destroying any hope of normal development.

A wisely disciplined child will grow into an adult who can handle himself or herself in private. When he's in a hotel and he can watch anything he wants, he learns to avoid X-rated channels because he learned self-control at home. Road rage isn't a problem for her because she learned to control herself from you. He knows that yelling and screaming during an argument will only bring heartache and regrets because he learned to guard his actions and watch his words when his emotions are running high. Your consistent, firm, yet loving discipline taught him those skills.

A child gains self-awareness from being known. A child gains self-control from being disciplined.

Third, *affirm your child's value*. This is more difficult than you might imagine because affirming a child's value without resorting to flattery will require discernment. My good friend Jim Dobson is a strong proponent of building a child's self-esteem, but many have twisted his counsel into something bizarre. For fear of wounding a child's self-image, teachers, coaches, and parents won't challenge him or her to excel. Poor performance as a result of little or no effort is typically met with gleeful cheers. A child is given compliments and affirmation that have no basis, which only seems to confuse him or her.

Flattery will amount to nothing ultimately. Instead, look for an authentic basis for compliments. Base your affirmation on characteristics that you genuinely see and truly admire. Reward real effort with encouragement, recognizing that his or her qualities and achievements will have child-sized proportions. To do this, you will have to know your son or daughter well. Furthermore, you will have to know what motivates your child, how much encouragement he or she will need, when to challenge him or her to try harder, and when it's appropriate to try something else.

The result for the parent is a growing respect for the child. The benefit for the child is he or she gains self-respect. And a child with a healthy respect for self will be prepared to enjoy healthy relationships as an adult.

As you determine to know your child's uniqueness, discipline yourself to set limits on his or her will, and affirm his or her value, take notes from the perfect Father. He knows you intimately, which puts Him in the best position to develop your maturity. He doesn't give you everything you want but never fails to meet your every need. And because He knows you, He knows the difference. His desire for you is that you grow into the kind of believer who enjoys the personality and the gifts He has given you, and He longs to see you fully alive. As the Lord develops your maturity, do the same for your child.

There are few responsibilities more rewarding than this . . . So don't wait to get started! Even if you've not done these things before, I urge you to begin. Remember, it's never too late to start doing what is right.

THREE

Establishing a Life of Self-Control

Frankie was a typical toddler, making life miserable for his mother just as he probably felt she was afflicting him. He was determined to do his thing; she had another plan; and so they were locked in a classic conflict of wills. Finally, having lost another battle to his adversary, little Frankie shuffled off to the dining room to be alone. He pushed a dining room chair over to a draped window, stood up on the chair, pulled the curtains back, and stared through the glass at the busy world outside.

Wise mothers know to check on toddlers who are too quiet for too long, so after some time had passed, Frankie's mother peeked into the dining room to see what he was up to. As she slipped quietly into the room, she heard him say in a low, quiet voice, "I have *got* to get out of here."

It's an age-old battle. As parents, we will often tire of the conflict. Nevertheless, we must remain consistent as we establish boundaries and maintain them with the rod and reproof. Our words and our actions must match so that our children will never have to struggle, trying to make sense out of a double message.

I write that even as I recall breaking that rule a number of times myself. I remember when our four were young and little Colleen became defiant on one occasion. Her mother said to me, "Either you take care of her or I will."

So I said to Colleen, "Get upstairs, young lady."

As she trudged up the staircase to her room, I could hear sniffles, and before I reached the top stair, *I* was choking back tears. (If you don't absolutely hate the thought of spanking your child, you need to reevaluate your motives.)

I followed her into her room and closed the door behind me. Her little round face turned up to mine, and I said, "Honey, you need to know something before this spanking. This hurts me a lot more than it does you."

She replied, "Well then, Dad, let's not do it. We'll both feel better."

So I didn't! I couldn't bring myself to do it. I said, "Promise me that you won't tell your mother I didn't spank you."

"I promise, Dad, I promise you . . . I'll never let her know."

Very often the problem is not strong-willed kids as much as their weak-willed parents. Without a clear message and steadfast consistency, how can a child learn? Ever try playing a game where the rules keep changing? It drives you mad.

I thought about this when Cynthia and I were touring Central Europe with a group from Insight for Living. We enjoyed an extended conversation with the man who was to drive our group from site to site. Before too long, we discovered that he was from Belgium and when he wasn't driving a tour bus, he was a professional dog psychologist! I said, "You're kidding. I've never met a dog psychologist before."

He said, "Yep, that's what I love to do. Really, though, I'm a dog owner's psychologist. I've rarely met a bad dog."

"Oh, really?" I said. "You haven't been in my neighborhood!"

He continued, "Seriously, I've rarely come across a bad dog. I see plenty of bad dog owners who handle their dogs all wrong. So I spend my time teaching dog owners how to train their dogs. I begin by telling them about the four essential elements for developing the behavior they want."

I still remember the four. First is knowledge: learning how dogs think. Second is time: if you don't spend adequate time with a dog, it will remain out of control. Third is consistency: the rules you established yesterday must apply today and every day, no exceptions. And fourth, patience: dogs will fail as they are being trained; they'll make messes. And then he made the comment, "You know, they're a lot like kids."

At that moment, it occurred to me that our major problem is not with kids being out of control. We have parents who have never helped their children get under control in the first place. Maybe you're one of them. If so, this chapter is for you.

ENDING YOUR FAMILY'S LEGACY OF SIN

We've learned that when God gives us a child, He doesn't hand us a piece of clay, waiting to be molded. The Lord crafted her with a set of gifts, strengths, a temperament, and a destiny. Each child is different, so we are to train her according to her way (*derek*), her characteristic manner.

We've also learned that each child is bent toward evil as a part of his or her nature. We are all born that way. We are sinners . . . by nature, by choice, and by birth. No part of us is untouched by this corruption, and that means we are separated from God. Only Jesus Christ can cure this fatal disease. We receive this healing by receiving Him by faith, trusting Him and Him alone for our restored relationship with God, the Father. A child needs a parent to teach him or her about the Savior. However, even after the Lord has taken up residence in the life of the child, his evil bent habitually incites him to rebellion—to doing things his own way. Charles Bridges wrote,

> Foolishness is the birthright of all [children]. . . . It means the very root and essence of sin in a fallen nature. . . . It includes all the sins of which a child is capable—lying, deceit, willfulness, perverseness, want of submission to authority—fearful aptness for evil, and a revulsion against good.[1]

This is true of each person, each child. It's true of you, me, and our children. Not only do they inherit a corrupt, sinful nature from us, but they also inherit a propensity to specific sins. In Exodus 34:6–7, God came to Moses in an awesome physical manifestation on Mount Sinai. Surrounded by cloud and light and noise that shook the ground, the Lord said,

> The LORD, the LORD God, compassionate and gracious, slow to anger, and abounding in lovingkindness and truth;

who keeps lovingkindness for thousands, who forgives iniquity, transgression and sin . . .

But then He continued with this chilling warning:

Yet He will by no means leave the guilty unpunished, visiting the iniquity of fathers on the children and on the grandchildren to the third and fourth generations.

Stop for a moment and take in the full meaning of that warning. I'll repeat it here: "He will by no means leave the guilty unpunished, visiting the iniquity of fathers on the children and on the grandchildren to the third and fourth generations."

Does that seem unfair to you? I will admit that it did to me as well, until I realized that my view of sin is the problem, not God's justice. We simply don't take sin seriously enough. When we do, we can be thankful that God, in His grace, stops at the third and fourth generations. The Hebrew word translated "visit" means "to number, visit, be concerned with, look after, make a search for, punish."[2] His warning is actually an expression of grace. Certain sins tend to run in the family. This is the Lord's promise to track them down and eliminate them in order to keep the sin from propagating from one generation to the next, growing stronger with each one. The human race could wipe itself out if He didn't do something to stop it.

Consider also the word "iniquity." This used to be a buzz word among religious types and has an old-timey ring to it. But it's an important theological term. The Hebrew word is *avon* (pronounced *ah-vown*, rhymes with "alone"), which has in mind the idea of distorting or twisting something out of its original shape. As we consider Exodus 34:7, the following is especially important and comes from the venerated *Theological Wordbook of the Old Testament*:

> [*Avon*] denotes both the deed and its consequences, the misdeed and its punishment . . . .
>
> The remarkable ambivalence between the meanings "sin as an act" and "penalty" shows that in the thought of the OT sin and its penalty are not radically separate notions as we tend to think of them. Rather in the OT the action of man and what happens to him are presupposed to be directly related as one process within the basic divine order.[3]

Sin has a ripple effect in families. Propensity to favor one particular sin might be handed from father to son genetically. One day science may prove or disprove this notion. However, we know for sure sins are passed from one generation to the next by example. Evidence of this emerges clearly in the historical books.

After David and Solomon ruled the united kingdom of Israel, Solomon's son Rehoboam ascended the throne. Due to his foolishness, the kingdom split, with the northern ten tribes siding with a former general, Jeroboam. This evil ruler was guilty of three types of iniquity: rebellion, idolatry, and sensuality. No fewer than fourteen times the biblical history books say that a northern ruler after him was guilty of "the sins of Jeroboam."

In Genesis 12, Abraham and Sarah found themselves living under the authority of a pagan king. This king saw that Sarah was a beautiful woman and he wanted her. So he inquired of Abraham how she was related to him. Abraham knew that if the king desired Sarah badly enough, the king might kill him. To save his own neck, he said to the king, "She's my sister." He lied. Later, in Genesis 20, Abraham found himself in a similar situation and lied to yet another king, saying, "She's my sister." Whenever Abraham felt threatened, he lied.

Abraham and Sarah had a son named Isaac. Isaac married Rebekah, who was, like Sarah, a beautiful woman. In Genesis 26, Isaac settled in a territory ruled by a pagan king, who noticed Rebekah's beauty. When asked about her, Isaac said . . . (You guessed it!), "She is my sister."

Isaac and Rebekah later gave birth to twins, Esau and Jacob. The story of Jacob is the story of a deceiver. He deceived his brother, he deceived his father (with the help of his mother), and he deceived his uncle. He fathered twelve boys, all liars—like their dad—except for Joseph. Abraham to Isaac, Isaac to Jacob, and Jacob to his sons, each generation passed on the sin of lying to the next. I'll bet, if you examined your own heritage, you would see a pattern too. Addicted parents produce addicted children. Brutal parents rear brutal sons and daughters. Deceivers beget deceivers.

I can trace impatience through my family tree. Cynthia can trace anger through hers. I remember studying this issue with Cynthia while our children were young, sitting at a table long into the night. Finally I said to her, "We have some longstanding tendencies we need to break. They need to stop with us and we need to prevent them from taking root in our children."

That's my challenge to you. Examine your own family history and look for harmful tendencies that affected you. Determine today to keep them from becoming a problem for your children. This examination will give you the insight, the wisdom, and the compassion you need to rescue your children from the sins that plagued you, and your parents, and theirs.

Applying "The Rod" Responsibly

Your first tool is knowledge. A second tool is "the rod."

"He who withholds his rod hates his son, but he who loves him disciplines him diligently" (Proverbs 13:24).

I will be considered politically incorrect in my style, and I know that many contemporary experts would not applaud my stand on corporal punishment, but I must stand on the authority of Scripture. This proverb and many others like it are too plain to ignore and too clear to confuse. These verses have been misused by people on both sides of the issue, but that does not invalidate the message of God's Word. We have a responsibility to discern its meaning and apply the principles reasonably and faithfully. That will be my task in this chapter.

In the previous chapter, I equated "the rod" to any form of physical correction, such as time-outs, grounding, removing privileges or property, allowing consequences to run their course, and spanking. In this chapter, I want to focus on "the rod" in its most literal sense: corporal punishment. It, like other parental measures, can be misused and overused. And I have seen it misapplied more often than not, so I understand why many oppose spanking as a form of discipline. Nevertheless, Scripture is plain, and in my experience, spanking is effective when applied within strict and appropriate guidelines.

Be Faithful and Consistent

"He who withholds his rod hates his son" (Proverbs 13:24). That's a tough statement, but it rings true when I hear adults tell me, "I wasn't very sure I was loved because my parents rarely enforced any rules." A good friend of mine, the late Billy Haughton, was in the process of rearing four daughters when he said to me, "You know, Chuck, I have learned that children can forgive you for almost anything except your failing to discipline them. That kind of neglect haunts them the rest of their lives." Billy was right. On the other hand, the second part of that verse says, "he who loves him disciplines him diligently."

Eugene Peterson's paraphrase renders the spirit of this statement well: "A refusal to correct is a refusal to love; love your children by disciplining them" (Proverbs 13:24 MSG).

A child feels loved when her parent is taking the time to correct her. A child who feels his parent's arms around him with a finger pointing to his chest feels secure. Children need to hear a parent say, "You're not going to get away with that" and to have that message reinforced with consequences. In the absence of that, they feel adrift—aimlessly connected to nothing and to no one.

Stay Clear of Abuse

I want to be especially clear about this subject. A distinct line separates abuse and physical discipline. We must know where that line is and be careful not to cross it under any circumstances. Here are five vital distinctions:

ABUSE IS CRUEL;

DISCIPLINE IS CORRECTIVE.

Applying punishment (of any kind) without a clear objective is cruel. Two questions must accompany any corrective measure: "What am I trying to teach?" and "What did my child learn?"

ABUSE IS UNFAIR;

DISCIPLINE IS FAIR.

Children nearly always feel that punishment is unfair, but two factors make the punishment fair. First, the boundary and the consequences were clearly spelled out beforehand, and second, the child was duly warned where possible.

ABUSE IS EXTREME (TOO LONG, TOO HARSH);

DISCIPLINE IS MEASURED (REASONABLE).

Clearly, this is a subjective judgment call, so accountability is key. Parental agreement will help, as will the opinion of a trusted friend, parent, or professional.

ABUSE LEAVES MARKS;
DISCIPLINE IS HARMLESS.

Bruises are off limits. Anything that leaves any kind of mark has gone too far. Spanking does not need to be overly applied to be effective. Be careful here. Restrain your anger.

ABUSE DAMAGES SELF-WORTH;
DISCIPLINE AFFIRMS SELF-WORTH.

The child will not feel especially good after a spanking; however, he or she should feel that the issue has been completely resolved. Abuse makes a child feel as if she is your enemy or that you dislike or resent her. Furthermore, abuse sends the message that the child is unworthy and therefore deserves to be harmed. Discipline says to the child, "This is necessary because I love you and I believe in you."

Never Punish Childish Irresponsibility

Dr. James Dobson makes the distinction between childish irresponsibility and willful defiance.

> There is a world of difference between the two. Understanding the distinction will be useful in knowing how to interpret the meaning of a behavior and how to respond to it appropriately. Let me explain. Suppose little David is acting silly in the living room and falls into a table, breaking several expensive china cups and other trinkets. Or suppose Ashley loses her bicycle or leaves her mother's coffeepot out in the rain. Perhaps four-year-old

Brooke reaches for something on her brother's plate and catches his glass of milk with her elbow, baptizing the baby and making a frightful mess on the floor. As frustrating as these occurrences are, they represent acts of childish irresponsibility and have little meaning in the long-term scheme of things. As we all know, children will regularly spill things, lose things, break things, forget things, and mess up things. That's the way kids are made. These behaviors represent the mechanism by which children are protected from adult-level cares and burdens. When accidents happen, patience and tolerance are the order of the day. If the foolishness was particularly pronounced for the age and maturity of the individual, Mom or Dad might want to have the youngster help with the cleanup or even work to pay for the loss. Otherwise, I think the event should be ignored. It goes with the territory, as they say.[4]

Never—ever—punish a child for immaturity. That's the place for instruction. A child spilling a glass of milk at the table never calls for discipline, never warrants a spanking. In fact, my brother, sister, and I turned over a glass at the table so often my dad felt that a meal wasn't complete without milk across his leg. So he'd occasionally tip a glass over for us!

Break the Will, Not the Spirit

We address irresponsibility with teaching; we address defiance with punishment. Defiance is not an *inability* to obey; it's a determined *unwillingness* to obey. It's the deliberate choice to ignore the will of an authority in favor of one's own. The purpose of punishment is to reestablish authority by temporarily breaking the child's will—teaching him or her to surrender when wrong—so that we can shape the will. We want children to have strong wills to keep them from becoming wishy-washy or pliable. However, their wills must recognize legitimate boundaries.

Our goal is *not* to break the child's spirit. We never want to see the light go out in a child's eyes. A hopeless child has no will at all. He or she has given up the possibility of pleasing Mom and Dad, knowing how to be successful, or feeling valued and loved. A broken spirit is the final result of a parent continually exasperating the child. Never go there.

APPLYING THE ROD WITH WISDOM

"Foolishness is bound up in the heart of a child; the rod of discipline will remove it far from him" (Proverbs 22:15).

"Do not hold back discipline from the child, although you strike him with the rod, he will not die. You shall strike him with the rod and rescue his soul from Sheol" (Proverbs 23:13–14).

The rod is a tool like any other. It has a proper application and it requires skill. Unfortunately, spanking has become taboo in our society, and to some degree, I understand why. Far too many parents overuse and misapply it, even some well-meaning parents. Corporal punishment should be used only to correct defiance and curb direct disobedience. Furthermore, spanking is not merely hitting. Too often I'll see a mom or dad lean down and say in a stern voice, "I *told* you not to do that . . . (swat)!"

The blow doesn't come as a lesson but as a punctuation mark. It's impulsive, rash, purposeless, often brutal, and only teaches the child to fear the parent. If your child begins to flinch when you assume a warning tone, spanking has damaged your relationship. The rod is a tool that has a specific purpose and it requires proper technique.

When I first began my study of the rod in Scripture, it sounded awfully harsh, so I thought a quick look at a Hebrew lexicon would ease my discomfort. It didn't. The word is often translated "club," which didn't help much! Actually, a rod can be a wooden stick of various thicknesses and lengths. In Scripture, it most often refers to a shepherd's staff or a royal scepter. In this context, "rod" points to a neutral instrument in the hands of authority.

Practically speaking, it's something separate and distinct from you. It's an implement, not your hand—and most certainly not your fist! Using an implement creates an important distinction in the child's mind, one that associates pain with the rod and less so with you, the parent. There's great value in that. It's something that's reasonably small and won't cause even temporary damage. I don't favor a switch pulled from a tree branch because it might cut. I wouldn't use a wooden spoon like some of my older relatives recall because it can easily bruise.

When our kids were little, we had a paddle-ball toy (it's a little wooden paddle with a ball attached by a long rubber band). We removed the ball and rubber band and we used the little, light paddle as an implement. I used to be a confirmed hand-paddler but soon discovered that the psychologists were right. One time, I spanked one of my daughters (using the method I'm about to describe) and put her to bed. I kissed her goodnight, clicked the light off, and closed the door. After about five minutes, I heard her crying out, "Daddy, come in here!" I rushed to her room to see what was wrong. I clicked on the light to see her pointing at the paddle. "Get that thing out of here!"

She wanted me but wanted nothing to do with the paddle. She associated pain with the implement, just as it should be.

Now, children have a certain area specially made for the paddle. Not the bottom of the legs and not the back. The fleshy part of the seat is the target. Never strike a child anywhere else for any reason. A slap across the face is humiliating and demoralizing, and it will only make the child angry—and for good reason. This is how to create distance and leave him or her with deep-seated resentment that could last for years. Furthermore, never discipline in public for the very same reasons.

Here are the steps I recommend when applying corporal punishment:

Explain the Offense

When you are calm, take the child aside and privately explain why he or she must receive a spanking. Your tone should be gentle and sympathetic, expressing genuine sorrow for what you *must* do. Remind him or her of when you clearly established the boundary and what the consequences would be.

"Remember when I said, 'Don't go swimming without me by the pool?'"

"Yes."

"What did I say would happen?"

"I'd get a spanking."

"I'm sorry, but you've left me no choice now. Do you understand that?"

Set the Time

Whenever possible, the spanking should take place immediately. If you are not in a place where that can be done in private, tell him or her when it will take place.

"As soon as we get home, I want you to go straight to your room. I'll be right behind you."

Apply the Rod

A paddling on the bottom should hurt—a lot—yet without causing damage. Aside from turning pink, there should be no marks—no lines or bruising. And the spanking should go on a little longer than the child expects. One hard swat isn't sufficient. Remember, this should be a rare and memorable event in a child's life.

Affirm the Child

When the spanking is over, set the paddle aside and sit down close to your child. He or she will often turn to you for comfort. Allow the crying to continue as long as the child wants while you continue to offer silent comfort in the form of hugs and caresses. Sometimes he or she will put on a little show to make you feel guilty. Don't react. Just sit quietly until your child's crying begins to subside. Then tell him how much you love him. Affirm his worth.

"You're such a wonderful daughter. I love you so very much."

"I'm so glad you're my son. That's why I couldn't overlook your disobedience. You are the best little boy in the world. I love you."

Avoid going back to the offense. Don't insist on an apology. He or she has paid a penalty for doing wrong, so forgiveness is not the issue. However, if the child offers an apology, accept it immediately and graciously. Leave all "preaching" to your pastor.

Close the Matter

Affirm your confidence in the child to do better next time, then prompt whatever comes next. If you are about to begin preparing dinner, ask if your child would like to help. Offer to read a story later. The point is to communicate to him or her that the relationship is secure and the matter is closed. Time to move forward with no lingering resentment. Put it behind you and never mention the incident again. *Never.*

As a child reaches the age of eleven or twelve, spanking needs to be set aside as a tool of instruction. Ideally, other forms of punishment will gradually displace it so that you find no need for spanking by that time. Besides, as children reach the teen years, paddling feels degrading and silly to them. You will gain much more by treating them as adults.

Four General Guidelines for Discipline

Let me close this chapter with four guidelines to keep in mind as you faithfully disciple your child. These apply to spanking but are appropriate for all forms of discipline.

Start Early

"Discipline your child while there is hope, but do not set your heart on causing his death" (Proverbs 19:18).

On Sunday, after I preached a message on discipline and the need to start early, a gentleman said to me, "I have three boys, two of whom are in prison. I've never heard anything like this before. Thank you for telling it as it is. I wish I had known. I, personally, never received this kind of discipline from my parents." He had been beaten, but never disciplined. He did not know how to curb his boys' bent toward evil while they were young. I urge you, start early.

Stay Balanced

Be sure to balance the rod with reproof. In fact, preface the rod with lots of verbal reproof first. Don't be too quick to reach for the paddle. This takes a great deal of time and patience, starting with knowledge of the child in whom you're striving to make a consistent investment. If you shortcut the process and apply the rod too quickly, you will encourage rebellion in your children rather than drive it from them.

Be Consistent

Clearly establish the boundaries and be sure your children understand the rules. Make certain all rules are consistent with all the siblings, making allowances for differences in age. And apply discipline faithfully. What was wrong and deserved a spanking yesterday needs to be considered wrong today and punishment must follow—even when you're tired, even if you've dealt with the same disobedience several times before on the same day.

Remain Reasonable

This could be an entire chapter on its own. Keep your expectations for the child appropriate for his or her age, and tailor your punishment accordingly. As one wise grandmother advised her daughter on childrearing, "Try not to see *everything*." Keep your cool. Anger not only frightens children, but it stops up their ears. They can't hear past your emotions; so if you want them to hear, speak quietly and act calmly.

Our ultimate goal in curbing willful, defiant behavior is to teach our children self-control. We all struggle with the desire to do our own thing and to follow any impulse that will gratify self. Maturity is, in part, the ability to control one's own impulses. When a child has an adequate measure of self-control, he or she is ready to receive instruction, more freedom, and greater privileges. Unless this first level of maturity has been reached, very little else we have to teach will have any effect. Self-control prepares the child to receive the next gift you have to offer: the gift of self-worth.

FOUR

Cultivating a Life of Self-Worth

For more than twenty-five years, I have passed along a twelve-word maxim to gatherings of believers all over the country. Twelve simple, powerful words that many who find themselves in the midst of transition find particularly helpful. A high school senior moving from home to begin life as an adult. A career-focused man or woman pursuing ministry late in life. A man or woman transitioning out of the military, with its order and structure, to the civilian world, which has far fewer guidelines. A parent launching his or her last child into the world and soon finding the house just a little too quiet.

But no one needs to hear these words more than parents in the process of rearing little children. The impact they have on a child under the age of ten is profound. These vital, fundamental words are important at any age but critical to little ones. Here they are:

KNOW WHO YOU ARE, ACCEPT WHO YOU ARE, BE WHO YOU ARE.

Does that seem too simplistic? Were you expecting something more profound? Before answering yes, answer this: are they true of you?

Pause and think about it. If you can claim that maxim, if you can support it with your actions, you are a rare individual. I tend to agree with Oscar Wilde on this point: "Most people are other people. Their thoughts are someone else's opinions, their lives a mimicry, their passions a quotation." Very few people can be genuinely themselves for two important reasons. First, very few people truly know who they are. Second, we live in world that is remarkably intolerant of individuality. The writer e. e. cummings described the fight well:

> To be nobody but yourself in a world which is doing its best, night and day, to make you everybody else, means to fight the hardest battle which any human being can fight; and never stop fighting.[1]

THE GIFT OF PERSONAL IDENTITY

I realize this may sound selfish to some, but let me assure you this has nothing to do with selfishness. It does, however, have everything to do with identity. This is having the self-assurance to stand for truth when everyone else fails to find the courage to do what they *know* to be right. This is having security enough to accept criticism with grace and to hear it as an opportunity for growth. This is having the ability to establish and maintain a healthy set of personal boundaries so that one can enjoy intimacy without reservation. It's having the guts to soar rather than cling-

ing to a familiar perch for years on end. I'm describing the difference between being an eagle and a parrot, as I wrote about a few
years ago in my book *Come Before Winter.*

> We're running shy of eagles and we're running over with
> parrots.
>
> Content to sit safely on our evangelical perches and
> repeat in rapid-fire falsetto our religious words, we are fast
> becoming overpopulated with bright-colored birds having
> soft bellies, big beaks, and little heads. What would help to
> balance things out would be a lot more keen-eyed, wide-
> winged creatures willing to soar out and up, exploring the
> illimitable ranges of the kingdom of God . . . willing to
> return with a brief report on their findings before they leave
> the nest again for another fascinating adventure.
>
> Parrot people are much different than eagle thinkers.
> Parrots like to stay in the same cage, pick over the same
> little pan full of seeds, and listen to the same words over
> and over again until they can say them with ease. They like
> company too. Lots of attention, a scratch here, a snuggle
> there, and they'll stay for years on the same perch. You and
> I can't remember the last time we saw one fly. Parrots like
> the predictable, the secure, the strokes they get from their
> mutual admiration society.
>
> Not eagles. There's not a predictable pinion in their
> wings! They think. They *love* to think. They are driven
> with this inner surge to search, to discover, to learn. And
> that means they're courageous, tough-minded, willing to

65

ask and answer the hard questions as they bypass the routine in vigorous pursuit of the truth. The whole truth.[2]

I'm not suggesting that all children must be daring thinkers in order to be healthy and whole. My point is that, as parents, we have the opportunity to help our offspring know their value, their worth, which gives them the confidence to become whatever God made them to be. If they don't learn it at home, they can easily become lost, confused victims of midlife crises. How rare are parents who deliberately give their child the gift of personal identity.

I came across a magnificent statement by cellist Pablo Casals:

Each second we live is a new and unique moment of the universe, a moment that will never be again. . . . And what do we teach our children? We teach them that two and two make four, and that Paris is the capital of France.

When will we also teach them what they are? We should say to each of them: Do you know what you are? You are a marvel. You are unique. In all the years that have passed, there has never been another child like you. Your legs, your arms, your clever fingers, the way you move.

You may become a Shakespeare, a Michelangelo, a Beethoven. You have the capacity for anything. Yes, you are a marvel.[3]

I want to challenge parents to remember, even rehearse these words. Start using them with your children. We can never know how important they might be when they someday find themselves alone in a big, lonely, intimidating world. Unfortunately, most children don't hear affirmation. They hear only criticism—hurtful words in a disapproving tone. Who knows what might emerge if we focus less on reprimands and criticism and zero in on what they do right?

Benjamin West, a brilliant painter who lived around the time of the American Revolution, began to explore his talent as a result of a remarkable incident involving his mother.

One day his mother went out leaving him in charge of his little sister, Sally. In his mother's absence he discovered some bottles of colored ink and began to paint Sally's portrait. In doing so, he made a very considerable mess of things with ink blots all over. His mother came back. She saw the mess, but said nothing. She picked up the piece of paper and saw the drawing. "Why," she said, "it's Sally!" and she stooped to kiss him. Ever after Benjamin West used to say, "My mother's kiss made me a painter."[4]

Be painfully honest here. Too many of us parents are far too mess-conscious to see the emerging artist. All we see are ruined carpets, stained clothes, cluttered desks, sticky fingers—one more unpleasant task added to an already busy day. We're so quick to see the depravity that we're blind to the marvel that God made and put in our care.

Now, I have to admit that in all my years of attending church, I have never heard a message on the value of self-worth from a conservative, evangelical pulpit. We're the ones who spend our time on sin and the solution (which deserves no less attention), but the problem is we ignore the dignity and beauty of humanity. Psalm 139 marvels at the Lord's creation of a person:

> For You formed my inward parts;
> You wove me in my mother's womb.
> I will give thanks to You, for I am fearfully and wonderfully
> made;
> Wonderful are Your works,
> And my soul knows it very well.
> My frame was not hidden from You,
> When I was made in secret,
> And skillfully wrought in the depths of the earth;
> Your eyes have seen my unformed substance;
> And in Your book were all written
> The days that were ordained for me,
> When as yet there was not one of them. (Psalm 139:13–16)

For those ready to pounce on me for daring to point out the good in people, go back and reread the previous chapter on depravity, the evil bent we all possess. I would remind you, however, that the Fall did not *erase* the divine image in man, nor does the doctrine of depravity *invalidate* human worth. David wrote Psalm 139 after the grotesque twisting of humanity's nature in the Garden, and he quite possibly wrote it after his own tragic moral failure. Nevertheless, He celebrates the beauty of humankind—and why not? For nine months, the Lord, in His creative genius, fashioned a little person to be absolutely unique, giving him or her a distinctive set of skills and unique abilities and special interests. He made that little person in His image, giving him or her a mind, a heart, a will, and a purpose: to know Him, love Him, obey Him, and to find a sense of fulfillment in His sovereign design.

Isn't that a marvel?

The stakes are higher than you might imagine. We have just a few short years with our children before they're off to school. Then they step onto that merciless playground where the whole system unloads on them with the implied message, "You had better fall in line if you don't want others to make fun of you." And it doesn't stop in grammar school. The pressure on a middle-school or senior-high student today has never been greater. One authority writes this about boys in particular:

> Now, more than ever boys are experiencing a crisis of confidence that reaches deep within the soul. Many of them are growing up believing they are unloved by their parents and are hated or disrespected by their peers. This results in a form of self-loathing that often serves as a prelude to violence, drug abuse, promiscuity, and suicide. It helps explain why both boys and girls do things that would otherwise make no sense, such as cutting their flesh, piercing sensitive body parts, tattooing themselves from head to toe, taking dangerous drugs, and/or identifying themselves with death, perversion, and satanic ritual. Some of them, it has been said, "cry with bullets."[5]

Hopefully, if we are successful as parents in helping our children know and accept themselves, they will be prepared to handle life in the adult world. For instance, a carload of fellow workers, visiting another city and looking to escape boredom, leaves the restaurant for the strip club. The security within a young man gives him the temerity to say, "No, thanks. That's not the way I live. You guys go ahead; I'll catch a cab to the hotel." He endures the ribbing and name calling, but he doesn't mind. He knows himself. His self-worth doesn't hang on their approval.

A young woman falls in love with the man of her dreams. He's handsome, successful, respected. But he hides a temperament that eventually surfaces as controlling and abusive behavior. One day, all that turns upon her and he calls her a vulgar, degrading name. Because she has confidence and a strong sense of worth and dignity, one time is enough. She's not so desperate for approval and love that she'll accept anything. With inner strength and firm confidence, she tells him that it's over. She may even give him the number of a place where he can heal and grow.

The issue of self-worth has deep significance for the child's spiritual growth as well. His or her relationship with Jesus Christ and the ability to become an authentic disciple depends upon it.

Many Christians . . . find themselves defeated by the most psychological weapon that Satan uses against them. This weapon has the effectiveness of a deadly missile. Its name? Low self-esteem. Satan's greatest psychological weapon is a gut-level feeling of inferiority, inadequacy, and low self-worth. This feeling shackles many Christians, in spite of wonderful spiritual experiences and knowledge of God's Word.

Although they understand their position as sons and daughters of God, they are tied up in knots, bound by a terrible feeling of inferiority, and chained to a deep sense of worthlessness.[6] The gift of personal identity will give your child the security to be a healthy adult and a genuine disciple.

BUILDING ONE ANOTHER

In Romans 14, Paul devotes a great deal of space to discussing the attitude we should have when someone engages in activity that we consider wrong or unwise, or at least questionable. In biblical days, meat sold at the public market quite possibly had been a part of worship in a pagan temple. The meat may or may not have been offered to idols. Nevertheless, Paul had no personal problem with eating it. As far as he was concerned, the idols were irrelevant because the gods they represented didn't exist; so the meat was no different than any other food. The greater danger facing the church was not sin-tainted meat but relational division. As a matter of conscience, some could not stomach the meat and thought less of those who could. Those who enjoyed the meat gave thanks for the provision but looked down with contempt on those who couldn't. In verses 1–12, he addresses the conflict, summarizing his thoughts in verse 10: "But you, why do you judge your brother? Or you again, why do you regard your brother with contempt? For we shall all stand before the judgment seat of God" (Romans 14:10).

First, let me clarify that the issue at hand is not a clear-cut moral right or wrong. In 1 Corinthians 5, Paul chastised the church for *not* judging the sinful actions of a young man and commanded them to put him out of the community until he repented. This, on the other hand, is a matter of conscience. Fine Christians today cannot agree on the wisdom of drinking wine or going to certain movies or sending their children to public schools.

For Paul, in the absence of clear, specific moral teaching from Scripture, the greater issue became peace between the sisters and brothers. The peace we are to pursue is embodied in the Hebrew concept of *shalom*. It's a community-fellowship kind of mutual acceptance. In Ephesians 4:1–3, he exhorts the community:

> Therefore I, the prisoner of the Lord, implore you to walk in a manner worthy of the calling with which you have been called, with all humility and gentleness, with patience, showing tolerance for one another in love, being diligent to preserve the unity of the Spirit in the bond of peace.

Paul challenged the Romans, struggling with honest, heartfelt disagreement over a practical matter of faith, to make one another the highest priority—even higher than having everyone agree with their own convictions. Take note of how they are to do this: "So then we pursue the things which make for peace and *the building up of one another*" (Romans 14:19; emphasis added).

Let me apply this verse to our purpose by paraphrasing it this way: Pursue the things which make for peace and the building up of your children rather than creating division by tearing them down with criticism.

Perhaps you weren't treated like that by your parents. Maybe your father was like mine. If I had spoken to my dad about self-worth, I think he would have looked at me as if I was from Mars. He simply didn't think in those terms. The only way he knew how to show love was to provide. His was a world of work. If you have energy, you work. If you have more energy, you do more work. If you have free time, you get another job. Life was not much more complicated than that for him. Once I understood that, it was okay. He was the best dad he knew how to be. But that's not the way I want my children to remember me, and that's not the kind of parents I want them to be. My desire is the same for you as it is for them—that you build up your children so that they know themselves, like themselves, and never fail to be themselves.

For many years, I have carried a slip of paper, now yellow with age, to gatherings on childrearing around the country. It contains a poem by an unknown author and it asks a penetrating question.

Are You a Builder?

I saw them tearing a building down,
A group of men in a busy town,
With a hefty blow and a zesty yell,
They swung with zest, and a side wall fell.

Asked of the foreman, "Are these men skilled?
The kind you would hire, if you had to build?"
He looked at me, and laughed, "No, indeed!
Unskilled labor is all I need.
Why, they can wreck in a day or two,
What it has taken builders years to do."

I asked myself, as I went my way,
Which of the roles have I tried to play?
Am I a builder with rule and square,
Measuring and constructing with skill and care?
Or am I a wrecker who walks the town,
Content with the business of tearing down?

Chances are fairly good that you're tearing your children down. The desire for them to be strong, well-mannered, successful children can be a strong one. So strong you may be focused only on fixing what's wrong, usually by pointing it out. And if we're brutally honest with ourselves, what's wrong is that they are not meeting our expectations for what we think they should be. You played sports, so your boy should. You were Phi Beta Kappa; therefore, your child should be. You had a vibrant social life, so your daughter should. You're musical, so your son should be too.

Perhaps you have one child who's a natural with the baseball, which pleases you because you love baseball. You share evenings together playing catch in the backyard. Then along comes another. He can't catch, he can't throw, and he wants to go back inside to read or listen to music. The temptation is to favor the child who is most like you and subject the one who isn't to comparisons. But neither favoritism nor holding one sibling out as an example for the others will alter what God ordained for each child.

Some kids love sports. Some are a whiz with puzzles and math. Some are messy and artistic. Some are structured and meticulous organizers. Some are dedicated students while others barely get by academically. Why? Because God made them that way. But if we're not careful, we'll see their God-ordained interests and temperaments as flaws to be fixed. We might even go so far as to make their differences moral issues to be disciplined, rather than hidden strengths to be developed.

How's the peace in your home? Are you a builder?

Signs of a Struggling Self-Worth

Some of the frustration you may be experiencing with your child may be the result of a sketchy sense of self or a poor self-image. Both can create problems for relationships and lead to very destructive—even self-destructive—behavior.

Defense Mechanisms

People with low self-worth erect defenses around themselves to keep from being discovered. They don't like what's inside, so they don't dare allow anyone else to see. They become aggressive or domineering. They feel the need to play moral or intellectual king of the mountain. Schoolyard bullies often grow up to become abusive to their families physically, mentally, and emotionally. Some carry it to work. The need to dominate doesn't have to be physical or emotional. It can be intellectual or spiritual. Even a pastor is not immune and can dominate a congregation.

The first biblical example that comes to mind is King Saul. He was tall and handsome—the picture of what everyone thought a king should be. The people idolized him until a young kid from the house of Jesse, who lived in the town of Bethlehem, slew a giant. Then the people sang, "Saul has slain his thousands, and David his ten thousands!" (1 Samuel 18:7). Saul tallied the score and his insecurity kicked in, big time. He had staked his self-worth on keeping the crown and receiving the adulation of his subjects. When David became a national hero, Saul sank into a deep depression. In the darkness of that mental state, demons afflicted his thinking and he tried to kill David, who escaped and fled into the wilderness. And for the next twelve years or more, Saul devoted considerable effort and expense to hunting David down. Why? Mostly because Saul was insecure. He couldn't abide someone else's success. But rather than take his insecurities to the Lord, he hid them behind his power.

Flimsy Boundaries

People with a poor self-image fail to set healthy boundaries, which leads them to accept abuse. They can also allow themselves to be stretched and pulled and pushed and overextended by people who have no intention to abuse them. But with such an overwhelming need for approval, people with no regard for self assume that acceptance means never saying no. Brennan Manning calls these people, including himself, "imposters."

Imposters are preoccupied with acceptance and approval. Because of their suffocating need to please others, they cannot say no with the same confidence with which they say yes. And so they overextend themselves in people, projects, and causes, motivated not by personal commitment but by the fear of not living up to others' expectations.[7]

People with low self-esteem allow the world to wipe its feet on them because they believe the voice in their heart that says, *I'm not worth anything more than this.*

However, people with a healthy sense of worth know their limits, communicate what they need, limit how far they will extend themselves, refuse to accept mistreatment, and take appropriate action when their boundaries are violated. Does that describe you? If so, chances are good you're cultivating those same qualities in the lives of your children. Good for you!

Masks

People who don't know or like themselves often wear masks in order to hide. They want to appear:

Strong: "I'll fight my way through life!"

Spiritual: "I'll learn the right vocabulary and quote the right verses."

Tough: "Nothing can affect me."

Cooperative: "Go with the people in power; don't make waves."

Lighthearted: "Keep them laughing so they won't look too deep."

Some of the funniest comedians were born and reared in horrific pain. "Jonathan Winters admits that his humor is a defense against childhood hurts. His parents divorced when he was seven, and he used to cry when alone because other children said he had no father. Winters now recognizes the wisdom of Thackeray's observation that 'Humor is the mistress of tears.'"[8]

Ironically, masks only prolong the agony. Proverbs 14:13 says, "Even in laughter the heart may be in pain, and the end of joy may be grief."

SIGNS OF A HEALTHY SELF-WORTH

The value of a healthy self-esteem cannot be measured. Someone who accepts and likes himself has the ability to love others unselfishly. Someone who believes she is worthy of compassion has compassion to give. Furthermore, accepting and liking who we are honors the God who created us. We validate the fact that He makes no mistakes and that we have worth just as we are.

A healthy self-image appears in four very important ways.

Self-Acceptance

People who have healthy self-esteems know who they are. They know what gifts they possess, what activities they enjoy most, and what pursuit gives them satisfaction. They are also equally aware of their limitations, and they don't think any less of themselves for having them. They accept themselves just as they are.

Security

People who know themselves and accept themselves are not threatened by those having more talent or more education or more money or more fame or more anything else. They feel no need to justify or defend themselves to any other human because they have their security in God, to whom they answer.

Contentment

Those who are secure in who they are as God made them are also content with the life they lead. They feel no pressure to perform for the sake of others or to maintain an image others may expect. They take appropriate pride in a job done "as unto the Lord." They are at peace with the place God has them and with the things He has provided.

Self-Aware

Self-accepting, secure, content people are very much in touch with their own feelings. They take ownership for their own emotions and feel no need to project them onto others or blame anyone for their anger, fear, or sadness. They experience the full range of human emotions, denying none and feeling all.

⟿

Sound good? Isn't that what we want for our children? Let me ask you, if you could give that to your children, would you care very much about what they did for a living? Isn't that the real measure of success for parenting?

CULTIVATING A CHILD'S SELF-WORTH

I want to underscore three practical suggestions for how you can build up your child and help him or her cultivate a robust, durable self-worth. I find them in Proverbs 4:20–27, the words of a father to his son.

Be Authentic

Become a model of authenticity.

> My son, give attention to my words; incline your ear to my sayings. Do not let them depart from your sight; keep them in the midst of your heart. For they are life to those who find them and health to all their body. (Proverbs 4:20–22)

The father pleads with his child to listen to his counsel and apply it. But for his words to have impact, the life of the parent must be transparent enough for the child to see and authentic enough to respect. Otherwise, our children see our spiritual walk for what it really is: a cliché. Tim Kimmel describes the concept this way:

> A cliché is a trite expression or idea that becomes meaningless with overuse. Clichéd also applies to words or actions that lose their punch or impact as a result of having no substantive connection to the bigger and more serious context in which they appear. Let me give you an example of standard clichés. Two friends run into each other on the

sidewalk, and they exchange a greeting that goes something like this:

"Hi, John. How are you?"

"Fine, Michael. How are you?"

"Fine."

What did these two men just say to each other? Nothing!"⁹

For our words to have substance, they must have life. Authentic, real, unvarnished, flawed experience. When we blow it, say, "I blew it." When we're wrong, say, "I was wrong." When we offend our children, we need to own the harm we caused and deliberately seek their forgiveness. When we are struggling with life, we need not hide all of it. Our children need to see us wrestle with problems, put our concerns before God in prayer, learn the lessons He has to teach, and overcome them in God's power—all before their eyes. Let them see your spiritual life as it is, warts and all. Children need to know that parents don't have all of life wired up tight.

Phony parents rear phony kids. So your first task may be to practice what you hope your child will learn. Know who you are, accept who you are, be who you are—authentic to the core.

Teach Authenticity

Watch over your heart with all diligence, for from it flow the springs of life. Put away from you a deceitful mouth and put devious speech far from you. Let your eyes look directly ahead and let your gaze be fixed straight in front of you. (Proverbs 4:23–25)

Note the progression: heart, speech, direction. It all starts with the heart. The Hebrew for the first sentence reads, literally, "More than all guarding, preserve your heart." This is the Hebrew way of overstressing a point. "First, foremost, and above all," he says, "guard your heart!"

The heart, for ancient people, was the seat of intellect, emotion, and will. It was the core essence of the person that involved much more than merely thinking. Too often our emotions and our actions are seriously out of step with our thinking, what we know to be right. The father in Proverbs 4 directs his child to examine the heart and protect it from pollution. If we do that, then our speech and our direction will have a much better chance of being what they should.

Encourage your children to be real. Teach authenticity by placing the highest value on the heart—more than saying the right things or even doing the right things. Lots of kids learn how to do that in Sunday school and Christian schools, then spin out of control once they leave home. Encourage them to be real. Don't teach them to protect their reputations or yours by avoiding what everyone will frown upon or by doing what will gain approval.

Many years ago, my good friend Ron Demolar operated a camp called Ponderosa at Mount Hermon in California, where he entertained middle-school kids from churches all over. Now, Ron's authentic to the core—he absolutely cannot stand clichéd Christianity and has a very mischievous sense of humor. He told me about one particular year and how he decided to set the tone for the rest of the week.

He said, "All these kids showed up and were so busy impressing each other with their spirituality that I thought I would break the ice with some simple little questions." He started with, "Hey kids, what's gray, runs real fast, has a big bushy tail, climbs trees, and hides nuts for the winter?"

The place was quieter than a room full of nuns. The kids just sat and stared. So he asked again, "Come on . . . what's gray, runs real fast, has a big bushy tail, climbs trees, and hides nuts for the winter?"

Finally, a little girl sheepishly put up a hand.

"Yes, go ahead," he said.

The girl hesitated, then said, "I want to say a squirrel, but I'll say Jesus Christ?"

That's the problem with what I call "hothouse religion." We don't learn how to grow and bear fruit; we just learn the right vocabulary and the right behavior and the right body language. We start sounding like everyone else in the hothouse, we stop seeing things the way they really are, and worst of all, we become *unreal.* Before you know it, the words have no meaning and we're all a bunch of phonies playing church. It doesn't fool the world, and—trust me on this—it doesn't fool our children!

Not only must we avoid being unreal, we must teach authenticity by being real and living what we believe. Tim Kimmel proposes this solution to the problem of clichéd Christianity and the horrific effect it has on our children's hearts.

When kids see parents who aren't resting on their laurels or coasting on their knowledge but are actively living a life committed to making an eternal difference every day, they are much more inclined toward a passionate relationship with Christ themselves. It will turn all they've learned from academics to action, from knowledge to wisdom, and from lessons to love. We need to show them how to serve and to encourage them to cultivate relationships with people who need a burst of light and a dash of salt. We need to help them pursue their spiritual passions. We need to help them see that Christ is to be pursued personally, not just academically.[10]

Reward Obedience

Let your eyes look directly ahead, and let your gaze be fixed straight in front of you. Watch the path of your feet and all your ways will be established. Do not turn to the right nor to the left; turn your foot from evil. (Proverbs 4:25–27)

This set of instructions is all about direction, what we often call walking the walk. It's about making progress through wise choices and avoiding the pain and sorrow that foolish choices bring. We must teach our children the value of walking straight ahead with God. We do that by working with them to set a goal, showing them how to work toward the goal using God-honoring means, and seeing that they reap the rewards of obedience.

You can also do this by being your children's loudest cheerleader. Applaud their independence, praise their initiative, and lavish your admiration upon them when they choose to stand alone against peer pressure. And when they fail, share a story of how you failed, how you suffered, learned, and grew.

THE RED PLATE

Years ago, Cynthia and I learned about an early American tradition that provides a tangible way to affirm the value of our children. It's called "The Red Plate." (It can be ordered online or purchased at many gift shops.) When you want to honor someone for a special day, a significant achievement, or simply to encourage him or her, set the table as you normally would, only place the red plate before the person of honor.

Not long ago, we took one of our now-grown daughters to dinner at her favorite restaurant because we wanted to give her something special that we wanted her to enjoy. She suspected nothing until the waiter brought her food on the red plate. Her reaction was not unusual. Her eyes immediately filled with tears. The full impact of this family tradition told her what we wanted her to hear without having to say one word: "You are very special."

She is, and our evening together was a great reminder of how valuable she is to both of us . . . and to God.

FIVE

Secret Struggles . . . Family Troubles

The dysfunctional family is not a recent discovery. When we examine the biblical record, we can trace it to the very beginning of human existence. Adam and Eve gave birth to two sons, Cain and Abel. Cain nurtured a petty jealousy for his brother's good standing before God, which sprouted into resentment and blossomed into hatred. Despite the Lord's warning, "Sin is crouching at your door" (Genesis 4:7), the root of hatred eventually led to the fruit of murder.

Isaac, son of the great Abraham, bore twins with his wife, Rebekah. Esau and Jacob fought in their mother's womb, wrestled for parental favor as children, grappled over the family fortune as young men, and fathered two nations that would be at each other's throats until the time of Christ and beyond. Herod the Great, a descendant of Esau, declared himself "King of the Jews" and, to safeguard his illegitimate hold on the throne, sought to kill the infant Jesus, Jacob's descendant. This was a family feud of epic proportions!

Jacob fathered twelve sons, including his favorite, Joseph. The young man's older brothers grew to hate him so much that they plotted his murder with genuine intent to carry it out. Only the begrudging conscience of one spared him. Instead of killing their brother, they stripped him and threw him into a dry cistern until a convenient slave trader took the problem off their hands for a tidy profit. To cover their crime, the brothers spattered Joseph's coat of many colors with goat's blood and convinced his father that he'd been devoured by a wild beast.

The levels and varieties of depravity in a family can stagger the imagination. And as the population expands, the sin grows increasingly prevalent. Now, in the twenty-first century, husbands mercilessly and sometimes fatally beat wives. Wives dominate and deceive their husbands and repeatedly cheat on them. Derelict dads and murderous mothers blaze across the headlines so often and so fast we forget their names and exchange sorrow for cynicism. The research of James Patterson and Peter Kim in their eye-opening book *The Day America Told the Truth* revealed that the most dangerous place in the world for American children is their own home! Children, caught in the deadly backwash of this bewildering dysfunction, have little hope of knowing what's supposed to be normal and, not surprisingly, repeat the awful cycle in their own families.

Perhaps what I've just described is your past. Maybe it's your present. Read on. There's help for you. If your family's interpersonal difficulties don't approach the level of abuse or dysfunction, I urge you also to read on. The principles we glean from Scripture will have application for you as well.

Two Timeless Truths

As we begin to examine this biblical story of physical and sexual abuse, let me assure you that my purpose is not to shock you or write something deliberately sensational. My motivation is to teach the Scriptures, which never glorify heroes. Unfortunately, included in the history of one of the world's most remarkable dynasties is an account of an appalling scandal that, tragically, occurs in families today. Our study of 2 Samuel 13 will immediately validate two timeless truths we instinctively know to be at work in the world.

First, *the worst acts of evil can be found in the most respected home.* There's no such thing as a perfect family. They don't exist. All families—famous or infamous, affluent or needy, black, Asian, white, Middle Eastern, interracial, churched, nonreligious, or pagan—they all struggle with selfishness and interpersonal strife. That's because 100 percent of all families are filled with people whose natures have been entirely corrupted by sin from the moment of conception. And some families, even those we would never suspect—powerful world leaders, pastors, intellectually gifted, respected corporate leaders—harbor the most shameful secrets.

George Washington said in 1786, "It is to be lamented . . . that great characters are seldom without a blot." Thomas Jefferson added a few years later, "None of us, no, not one, is perfect, and were we to love none who had imperfections, this world would be a desert for our love." Theodore Roosevelt offered these encouraging words in 1916: "It is not having been in the Dark House, but having left it, that counts." My hope is that today, you will find the courage to leave the Dark House, which has too long held you captive.

Second, *unresolved evil leads to consequences that fester and cause more complications.* As unresolved evil festers, it causes debilitating psychological issues such as fear, nightmares, panic, paranoia, depression, anger, and even physical illness. As the evil spreads, it complicates relationships within the family, distorting one's ability to be appropriately intimate or twisting the spirit to the point of rage and acts of violence. And worst of all, the sin can be perpetuated as the wounded soul becomes a villain to yet another generation of innocent victims.

My sincere hope is that if you are caught in the trap of physical or sexual abuse—either as a victim or as the perpetrator—you will not wait to finish this chapter before seeking help. Sins—especially sins like abuse—never solve themselves. They only fester and cause future complications.

If, on the other hand, your home is presently free of dysfunction, don't be too quick to discount the possibility. Abuse and other extreme forms of family trouble aren't always the result of prior dysfunction in the parents' homes. I don't write that to alarm you, only to encourage you to take the possibility seriously so that you will respond promptly and appropriately to evil when it appears.

The Shameful Drama

Second Samuel 13 exposes a royal scandal that involves David, Israel's most famous king, and several other people in his family you may not know. Before I set the stage and introduce the characters, let me assure you that my purpose is not to be severe or overly judgmental with David. Space does not permit me to convey the deep admiration and respect I have for his example of leadership, personal strength, integrity, and unquestioned devotion to the Lord. We should all aspire to be a man or woman of God as David was. Nevertheless, we must keep George Washington's words in mind: ". . . great characters are seldom without a blot." David's character, like mine and yours, had some very significant blots. The Holy Spirit inspired the human author to include these unflattering details for our benefit, so that we can observe where David failed in his role as father and avoid the heartbreak that eroded his family relationships and ultimately fractured his nation. We best honor heroes by rising above their failings.

David

In 1 Samuel 13:14 the Lord described David as a man after His own heart. He was a courageous warrior, a prolific poet, a generous king, a magnetic leader, a remarkable administrator, a sensitive servant of God . . . and a polygamist. In the ancient world, having a collection of wives was not only a symbol of power, but it was expected of a king. But God established a higher standard for Israel's kings, forbidding them to maintain a harem. Unfortunately, David chose to ignore what must have seemed to him an insignificant restriction and to indulge his sexual appetite. This decision would have no small effect on his family and, as a result, the entire kingdom. Alexander Whyte wrote:

91

Polygamy is just Greek for a dunghill. David trampled down the first and the best law of nature in his palace in Jerusalem, and for his trouble he spent all his after-days in a hell upon earth. David's palace was a perfect pandemonium of suspicion, and intrigue, and jealousy, and hatred—all breaking out, now into incest and now into murder.[1]

The Bible gives us the names of eight wives besides the unknown number of other wives and concubines, all of whom had children by David (see chart on next page). By the time of this scandal, he had recovered from his moral fall with Bathsheba, which involved the murder of her husband, David's longtime friend Uriah. He had repented, the Lord had forgiven him, and the great king was again Israel's champion against her enemies. However, David's moral fortitude had lost its old passion. Shame for his own sin apparently made him tentative in prosecuting the sins of others, an important function as king of Israel.

The earlier scandal also took its toll in other ways. Until his sin with Bathsheba, David had never experienced defeat on the battlefield. His success was phenomenal. Some scholars estimate that he expanded Israel's territory from six thousand square miles to sixty thousand. The Lord forgave David's sin and restored their intimate relationship; however, in His inscrutable sovereignty, He would allow the consequences of the king's choices to unfold. In 2 Samuel 12:10–11, the Lord declared, "Now therefore, the sword shall never depart from your house, because you have despised Me and have taken the wife of Uriah the Hittite to be your wife.

THE FAMILY OF DAVID
1 Samuel 18:27; 1 Samuel 25:42–43;
2 Samuel 3:3–5; 1 Chronicles 3:1–9; 14:3–4

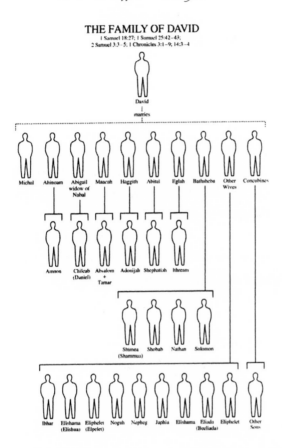

. . . Behold, I will raise up evil against you from your own household."

The events of 2 Samuel 13 follow closely on the heels of this declaration.

Amnon

While on the run from Saul, David married Ahinoam, with whom he had his first son, Amnon. The lad spent his early years in Hebron, where David had only two wives. As the king's power grew, so did his harem. Amnon's earliest memories included watching his father collect women for the sake of sating his sexual appetite.

Jonadab

Wherever there's conflict, you'll find a political weasel playing each person against the others. Yet somehow he's everybody's friend. Jonadab was just such a man. As a nephew of David by his brother, he was a close relative in the royal court. But because he was not in line for the throne, he had little power, which made him particularly dangerous.

Absalom

Talmai, the king of an important city 150 miles north of Jerusalem, gave his daughter Maacah to David as his third wife. David and Maacah gave birth to at least two children, Absalom and his younger sister, Tamar. By the time of the events of 2 Samuel 13, David had moved his capital to Jerusalem, conquered vast territory, committed his sin with Bathsheba, and fathered Solomon. In the midst of all this domestic mess, Absalom grew to be a man with a household of his own and a substantial income from the flocks he had acquired.

As I read about the life of David, his many conquests, his organization of the nation, his diplomacy, his involvement in the matters of worship, and his many, many wives, it occurs to me that he had time enough to conceive children but very little left for rearing them. Amnon and Absalom effectively had no father.

Tamar

Absalom's mother bore a beautiful daughter with David. Her beauty was the talk of the palace. We know from the story that Tamar was unmarried and, therefore, a virgin, most likely living in the care of her father's household. She, too, grew up seeing the relative value of women and endured the unruly atmosphere of the royal house. Alexander Whyte described Amnon, Absalom, and Tamar's environment this way: "A little ring of jealous and scheming parasites, all hateful and hating one another, collected around each one of David's wives."[2] Their influence extended to the children.

THE VILE PLOT

The story begins with the innocuous phrase, "Now, it was after this . . ." 2 Samuel 13 occurs after David's first children have become adults, after his fall with Bathsheba and subsequent restoration, and immediately following a promising victory over Israel's perpetual enemy, the Ammonites. Take note of how the human author relays the order of events:

- The Lord said, "I will raise up evil against you from your own household."
- David comes out of mourning.
- Solomon is born.
- David conquers a stubborn enemy.
- David returns from the battlefield as a conquering king.

95

The good fortune and pleasant circumstances would seem to suggest that David's family troubles were largely over. However, the lifestyle of sexual excess, cultivated over a thirty-year period before the eyes of his children, set in motion a bizarre chain of events. Eugene Peterson's paraphrase illuminates the subtleties of the setting.

> Some time later, this happened: Absalom, David's son, had a sister who was very attractive. Her name was Tamar. Amnon, also David's son, was in love with her. Amnon was obsessed with his sister Tamar to the point of making himself sick over her. She was a virgin, so he couldn't see how he could get his hands on her. (2 Samuel 13:1–2 MSG)

Amnon lusted after his half sister (same father, different mother), and he wanted her for one thing: sex. In fact, he nearly drove himself mad fantasizing about her body. Ordinarily, he could have sated his lust as his father had; marry her and have his way until he was bored. But she was his half sister, so marriage was out of the question in that Jewish home. Ah, but lust will find a way. Amnon's cousin Jonadab had a solution: rape her.

> Jonadab then said to him, "Lie down on your bed and pretend to be ill; when your father comes to see you, say to him, 'Please let my sister Tamar come and give me some food to eat, and let her prepare the food in my sight, that I may see it and eat from her hand.'" So Amnon lay down

and pretended to be ill; when the king came to see him, Amnon said to the king, "Please let my sister Tamar come and make me a couple of cakes in my sight, that I may eat from her hand."

Then David sent to the house for Tamar, saying, "Go now to your brother Amnon's house, and prepare food for him." (2 Samuel 13:5–7)

Tamar was innocent. She merely obeyed the order of her father, completely unaware of the plot. Later details reveal that she was, in fact, very virtuous.

So Tamar went to her brother Amnon's house, and he was lying down. And she took dough, kneaded it, made cakes in his sight, and baked the cakes. She took the pan and dished them out before him, but he refused to eat. And Amnon said, "Have everyone go out from me." So everyone went out from him. Then Amnon said to Tamar, "Bring the food into the bedroom, that I may eat from your hand." So Tamar took the cakes which she had made and brought them into the bedroom to her brother Amnon. When she brought them to him to eat, he took hold of her and said to her, "Come, lie with me, my sister." (2 Samuel 13:8–11)

Perhaps this makes too much of the details, but I cannot help but notice that Amnon's clutching of his sister came with an invitation. Could it have been that his mind was so twisted by lust and such an absence of morality that he actually thought she might return his advance?

Take note of the complete contrast in Tamar's character to that of her brother. I am very impressed by her wise, reasoned, and even gentle response. These are the words of a woman sincerely interested in protecting her brother's innocence as well as her own.

> But she answered him, "No, my brother, do not violate me, for such a thing is not done in Israel; do not do this disgraceful thing! As for me, where could I get rid of my reproach? And as for you, you will be like one of the fools in Israel. Now therefore, please speak to the king, for he will not withhold me from you." However, he would not listen to her; since he was stronger than she, he violated her and lay with her. (2 Samuel 13:12–14)

Her last plea, "Please speak to the king," I find especially heartrending. Some have suggested that either the laws forbidding this marriage were not followed or that Tamar was ignorant of the law. But I hear above all the desperate words of a panicked young woman trying to keep from being raped, then fighting to preserve her virginity, a quality having staggering significance in her time and culture.

Nevertheless, Amnon brutally raped his half sister, and his reaction becomes the first of several startling contrasts.

Then Amnon hated her with a very great hatred; for the hatred with which he hated her was greater than the love with which he had loved her. And Amnon said to her, "Get up, go away!" (2 Samuel 13:15)

Tacitus, the ancient historian, wrote, "It is, indeed, human nature to hate the one whom you have injured." [3] In my years as a pastor, I have discovered that intense guilt produces either genuine repentance or alarming hostility, rarely anything in between. Despite her pleas, Amnon wasted no time throwing Tamar into the street after having used her as an object for sex. To him, the beautiful, innocent Tamar was not a person, but a thing to be used and then tossed aside.

Then he called his young man who attended him and said, "Now throw this woman out of my presence, and lock the door behind her." Now she had on a long-sleeved garment; for in this manner the virgin daughters of the king dressed themselves in robes.

Then his attendant took her out and locked the door behind her. Tamar put ashes on her head and tore her long-sleeved garment which was on her; and she put her hand on her head and went away, crying aloud as she went. Then Absalom her brother said to her, "Has Amnon your brother been with you? But now keep silent, my sister, he is your brother; do not take this matter to heart." So Tamar remained and was desolate in her brother Absalom's house. (2 Samuel 13:17–20)

In the ancient Hebrew culture, people in mourning put ashes on their heads and tore their clothes. It was a sign of deep distress over a personal loss. When Job experienced the death of his children and the loss of everything, including his health, he tore his tunic and poured ashes over his head (Job 1:20). Tamar lost something very precious to her.

Take note of Absalom's response to Tamar's grief. Upon seeing his sister's torn robe and ashen head, his mind immediately went to Amnon. He probably knew of David's request and had, no doubt, seen the lust on Amnon's face (men rarely miss this), and he put the clues together. As much as Absalom loved his sister—so much that he later named a daughter after her—he probably contained his rage only for the sake of the justice he was sure his father would execute.

Some have suggested that Absalom's words to Tamar were callous or that he minimized her anguish. Admittedly, in English and without the benefit of an ancient perspective, his words could appear flippant. However, his later actions reveal that what happened to her was deadly serious to him. In the context of this story, it is far more likely that his words were meant to reassure his sister, who was understandably hysterical. His words reflect his confidence in the patriarchal system of justice that ruled Hebrew society.

"But now keep silent, my sister" = Calm down; everything will be resolved in due course.

"He is your brother" = Because this matter is not complicated by the politics of dealing with another patriarch's family, justice will be swift and sure.

"Do not take this matter to heart" (literally, "Do not put your heart to this matter") = Don't consider your life over; justice will roll down and vindicate you.

In those days, the family dispensed justice when one of their own committed a crime. If a person committed an offense against someone outside the family, his patriarch was expected to hold him accountable. If the patriarch refused to do this, the offended family appealed the matter to the king, who would mercilessly enforce the law. In this case, the patriarch for both Tamar and Amnon was also the king. Absalom had every reason to expect that David would execute justice swiftly.

THE MURDEROUS PLOT

As a son, Absalom hoped that his dad would care enough about Tamar to step in. Children need parents to protect them, to face difficult truths with them, and do what is right, even at great personal cost. They need a hero. They need someone to believe them when they reveal abuse at the hands of another family member or a close friend of the family. They desperately hope that someone will hear them and will become their champion— a protector, an advocate, a guardian. In this case, two family members conspired to rape another. This was a time to stand in defense of the innocent, the helpless, not to protect the reputation of the family or the interests of the favored perpetrators.

While Absalom waited for justice, Tamar took refuge in his household . . . not the palace.

"Now when King David heard of all these matters, he was very angry" (2 Samuel 13:21).

That's it. End of discussion. Over and out. Read on and you'll be disappointed—even shocked—to find that nothing more was said or done by David concerning the rape of his daughter by his son . . . only a flash of anger. Given his own recent past—adultery with Bathsheba, the murder of his friend Uriah, the public humiliation, the ruined reputation—we can appreciate how tentative he might have been to judge the sins of another. Furthermore, the Septuagint, the Greek translation of the Hebrew Scriptures, adds the note: "But he did not grieve the spirit of Amnon his son, because he loved him, since he was his firstborn."[4] Eugene Peterson's paraphrase, *The Message*, reads, "King David heard the whole story and was enraged, but he didn't discipline Amnon. David doted on him because he was his firstborn."

This passivity on David's part was nothing new. First Kings 1:6 describes his handling of Adonijah this way: "His father had never crossed him at any time by asking, 'Why have you done so?'" The literal Hebrew reads, "He did not correct him from his days," which means "from the earliest days—ever in his life." David was a passive father to Adonijah, so we can be reasonably certain he was passive toward his family in every way. Tragic.

David's flash of anger probably encouraged Absalom. So he waited. A week went by. Then a month. Six months. Though frustrated with his father's passivity, Tamar's protector perhaps thought that the need for justice would eventually begin to eat his father's soul as it did his own. A year. Tamar's worst fears proved to be justified. Eighteen months. In the meantime,

Absalom avoided Amnon because of the deep hatred he harbored. Still nothing from David. Two years . . . think of it.

After two full years, David's anger had long since passed and it became clear to Absalom that his father would do nothing to bring Amnon to justice. David had moved on to what he knew best: conquering, composing, administrating, building. Perhaps he thought the problem would solve itself. But remember our second principle? *Unresolved evil leads to consequences that fester and cause more complications.*

Just as David began to feel secure about having avoided another scandal, Absalom's seething anger against his father was about to threaten everything David had built. While we can't excuse the young man's actions, we can appreciate his motive: vindication for helplessly humiliated Tamar. Absalom woke each morning to see his sister's "desolation." Night after night, he heard her cry herself to sleep—for two, long years, even as Amnon enjoyed the hope of a bright future as Israel's next king. Enduring such passivity must have been excruciating.

"Now it came about after two full years that Absalom had sheepshearers in Baal-hazor, which is near Ephraim, and Absalom invited all the king's sons" (2 Samuel 13:23).

Sheep-shearing season was a time for feasting and celebrating among the ancient Hebrews. Shearing the wool from thousands of sheep required lots of temporary labor over many days, so they turned the occasion into a festival. It was also a time for the owner to share his wealth with family and friends. In this case, Absalom wanted his shearing festival to be a big family gathering . . . but a murderous plot was brewing.

Absalom came to the king and said, "Behold now, your
servant has sheepshearers; please let the king and his
servants go with your servant." But the king said to
Absalom, "No, my son, we should not all go, for we will
be burdensome to you." Although he urged him, he
would not go, but blessed him. Then Absalom said,
"If not, please let my brother Amnon go with us." And
the king said to him, "Why should he go with you?"
(2 Samuel 13:24–26)

I find several intriguing tidbits in this passage. First,
Absalom wanted the entire family present at whatever he had
planned, including his father. Second, when David declined,
feeling his presence would be too much of a financial burden,
Absalom specifically named Amnon in his next request. Could
this have been his way of gauging his father's reaction? If so,
David's blank stare let him know that he failed to connect the
dots . . . the passive father had forgotten the entire matter.

After some convincing, David agreed to allow all of his sons
to attend Absalom's celebration. Perhaps he thought Absalom
had gotten over his anger.

Absalom commanded his servants, saying, "See now, when
Amnon's heart is merry with wine, and when I say to you,
'Strike Amnon,' then put him to death. Do not fear; have
not I myself commanded you? Be courageous and be
valiant." (2 Samuel 13:28)

Amazing! Although we shouldn't be surprised. The sin of the father passed to the son. This only reinforces our earlier point that sin never resolves itself. Sin must be fully revisited and addressed.

> The servants of Absalom did to Amnon just as Absalom had commanded. Then all the king's sons arose and each mounted his mule and fled. Now it was while they were on the way that the report came to David, saying, "Absalom has struck down all the king's sons, and not one of them is left." Then the king arose, tore his clothes and lay on the ground; and all his servants were standing by with clothes torn. (2 Samuel 13:29–31)

When King David heard the rumor that *all* of his sons were killed, the political weasel Jonadab made sure he was in the right place at the right time. Take note of how he chose to deliver the news.

> Jonadab, the son of Shimeah, David's brother, responded, "Do not let my lord suppose they have put to death all the young men, the king's sons, for Amnon alone is dead; because by the intent of Absalom this has been determined since the day that he violated his sister Tamar. Now therefore, do not let my lord the king take the report to heart, namely, 'all the king's sons are dead,' for only Amnon is dead." (2 Samuel 13:32–33)

Clever. He very likely knew of the plot (weasels always have the best gossip), yet he did nothing to stop it. He made sure he was close at hand so he could be the bearer of good news to David in the midst of his tragedy. And Jonadab's choice of words give the impression he thought the rape of Tamar was deplorable, yet we know that he played a central role in the crime—it was his idea!

> Now Absalom had fled. And the young man who was the watchman raised his eyes and looked, and behold, many people were coming from the road behind him by the side of the mountain. Jonadab said to the king, "Behold, the king's sons have come; according to your servant's word, so it happened." As soon as he had finished speaking, behold, the king's sons came and lifted their voices and wept; and also the king and all his servants wept very bitterly.
>
> Now Absalom fled and went to Talmai the son of Ammihud, the king of Geshur. And David mourned for his son every day. So Absalom had fled and gone to Geshur, and was there three years. (2 Samuel 13:34–38)

After Absalom took the law into his own hands, having Amnon executed, he fled to a city ruled by his maternal grandfather. Clearly, Absalom's act of hatred against Amnon was also directed to his father, who had never dealt with the horrible sin against his precious daughter. Observe the deep emotion felt by David: "the king and all his servants wept very bitterly," and "David mourned for his son every day." Yet we see no action.

The very next verse begs an important question, which punctuates David's passivity with a giant exclamation point.

"The heart of King David longed to go out to Absalom; for he was comforted concerning Amnon, since he was dead" (2 Samuel 13:39).

If David's heart longed to go out to Absalom, why didn't he? The kingdom of Geshur lay fewer than a hundred miles to the north of Jerusalem, just to the east of the Sea of Galilee. There Absalom remained in exile with his grandfather for three years, during which time David made no attempt to restore their relationship. In the next chapter, he permitted Absalom to return to Jerusalem but refused to see him for another two years. When Absalom pressed the issue, David's welcome could only be described as cool.

David's disconnect between his feelings and his actions, which kept him from addressing the sin in his family, eventually caught up with him. We'll study this in detail in the next chapter. Absalom led a successful revolt, took his father's throne, and expelled him from the country. Only after a very bloody civil war and the violent murder of Absalom did David regain his kingdom.

As we close our study of this ancient dysfunctional family's struggles and troubles, let me return to the two timeless truths before offering three principles for today. Let them sink into your mind in such a way that you'll never forget them.

THE WORST ACTS OF EVIL CAN BE FOUND IN THE MOST
RESPECTED HOME.

- AND -

UNRESOLVED EVIL LEADS TO CONSEQUENCES THAT FESTER AND CAUSE MORE COMPLICATIONS.

THREE WARNINGS FOR PASSIVE PARENTS

In my fifty-plus years in pastoral ministry, I have seen secret struggles and family troubles that would boggle the mind. I wish I could say that the Bible's portrayal of David's difficulties was extreme for the sake of making an impression, but it's not. The destructive power of sin left unchecked can do the same, and worse, in any family.

Plain and simple, David's fatal flaw as a parent was his passivity. He conquered nations and built the kingdom, but he left his family to solve its own problems. But children can't rear themselves. They need more than food, water, and shelter; they need us—actively engaged parents who stay in touch.

Let's be honest with ourselves—we can identify with David's passivity. We're guilty too. David's story lets us see the potentially deadly result of passive parenting, even in the home of an otherwise superb leader and sensitive man of God. His experience also points to no fewer than three warnings for any parent who might be tempted to neglect his or her role as protector and guide.

First, *disconnected and damaged relationships at home result in dysfunctional family members.* To you who are in the process of rearing children, I urge you to cultivate genuine closeness within the family to prepare your children to be healthy adults having the capacity to enjoy wholesome relationships. This requires a willingness to face difficult truths and follow through with decisive action. Let's face it, we usually know what to do to keep relationships on track or to restore them when they crash, but we lack the courage to follow through. The gap between knowing and doing caused immeasurable misery in the royal household, producing at least three dysfunctional sons: Amnon, Adonijah, and Absalom.

Tim Kimmel, in his fine book *Why Christian Kids Rebel* writes,

> It's a strange thing about our personal sins. When our kids move away and we haven't resolved our sins of commission or omission with them, these childhood disappointments grow larger and larger until they dominate our kids' focus and dictate many of their actions. In fact, our unwillingness to try to make peace with our kids before they leave home can set them up for a lifetime of bad decisions.[5]

To parents of adult children: they've left the nest, they're on their own, and they move from one dysfunctional relationship to another. Perhaps you feel partially responsible because your home was a poor model. Maybe you committed or permitted (they are close to being the same) abuse and neglect. Do not ignore the past failure! Go back. You may need to arrange for someone trained in Christian counseling to help facilitate the process, but please go back. You may have to hear some things that will be difficult for your children to say and painful for you to accept. You may need to say some things you have never said before. Nevertheless, doing nothing will only prolong the anguish and give sin more opportunity to spawn more complications.

Don't be fooled by the silence as David was. After two years of calm, he thought the issue had resolved itself. But unresolved sin never works itself out.

Second, *passive and permissive parents produce angry, frustrated children.* Much of the problem can be traced to our habit of staying too busy. As Peter Marshall once wrote, "We're in such a hurry, we hate to miss one panel of a revolving door." We're so busy, so driven to complete the next task at the office or the church, we barely have time to think of relationships at home. Yet, I ask you, how many of your fondest memories involve a task well done? Chances are, none of your memories involve a task at all. A life well lived is composed of memories, not a completed checklist. Memories are made from moments in time, not tasks.

If we're brutally honest with ourselves, we have to admit that the problems our children present to us can feel like tasks added to an already overburdened list. So we prioritize our days, listing unpleasant items near the bottom, resolving to give them due attention if they begin to approach a crisis level. Meanwhile, the child hears the message we have sent: *You are less important than the project I must complete by next Wednesday.* No wonder they become bitter.

If you find yourself living with angry and frustrated kids, instead of blaming them, look within. Don't look for someone to blame, least of all your children. Look deep within yourself.

How I wish that David would have faced the difficult truth

and dealt with it! I think of his strength, his wisdom, his leadership, his sensitivity, his influence . . . had he invested all of those great qualities in his sons, the story would have been much different. Amnon needed to hear from the beginning, "Son, I've made a mess of my life by allowing my desire for women to run unchecked. Don't let it consume you, or it will lead to disaster. I must not allow it to continue."

Tamar needed her father to be her protector. Absalom needed him to uphold righteousness and punish Amnon's sin. But David checked out. He remained passive, aloof, preoccupied with the affairs of state. Consequently, Tamar withered and despaired. Absalom grew vengeful to the point of murder. I realize that part of us secretly applauds Absalom for doing the job David should have done. But I must remind you that by the time of the murder, Absalom's motive had turned from appropriate justice to personal hatred. As we'll see in the next chapter, his bitter hatred knew no limits.

I repeat, if your children are angry and frustrated, look within. Have you remained passive or uninvolved despite the troubles you have seen brewing in them? You may not know what to do. Do *something*. Seeking wise counsel would be a good place to begin. But do *something*.

Third, *unresolved and unreconciled conflicts create wounds that never heal themselves*. Conflicts must be resolved. The truth must be sought and shared. Wrongs must be acknowledged and repented of. Closure must be pursued and agreed upon. Otherwise, you leave a wound that never quite closes. Your children may never turn bitter or seek revenge as aggressively as

Absalom did, but they will never be fully themselves with you. Furthermore, your relationship will never go deeper than the freshest injury—cordial, perhaps even pleasant, but it will forever lack depth.

If you find that family members are distant, don't assume that because you feel fine that they are okay. Reach out. Allow them to uncover that weeping, tender wound. Don't be afraid to look at it. Defensiveness, self-protection, or attempts to explain your intentions are like pouring acid on it. Instead, offer empathy, defend nothing, and ask forgiveness. Your vulnerability will be a healing salve to your wounded family member. And I guarantee, once the wound begins to heal, you will be surprised by the grace you receive—far more satisfying than the justification you presently offer yourself.

May I remind you? It's never too late to start doing what is right.

⌒

I hope that you will take some comfort in the first timeless truth and that it will give you courage. *The worst acts of evil can be found in the most respected home.* I also hope you will take the second truth seriously. *Unresolved evil leads to consequences that fester and cause more complications.* Deliberately resist these common rationalizations:

- "He's the one who owes me an apology! The first move is his."

- "When she wants to get serious about this relationship, I'm here. I'll wait her out."
- "This is not a big deal; it'll resolve itself if I give it time."
- "Hey, nobody's perfect. Compared to _____, I'm doing pretty well."
- "That's ancient history; nobody even remembers it. Why dig up old trouble?"
- "Everybody in our family is a Christian. Each person can take his wounds directly to the Lord."

All of those statements can be followed with the same one-word response: *Wrong!*

The first step is *yours.* Take it.

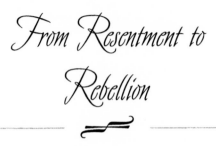

SIX

From Resentment to Rebellion

E verybody loves a good story. As most of us know, the Bible is full of them. Stories of love, hate, grace, revenge, rejection, and redemption. And stories of parents and children are woven into the fabric of the Scriptures. Two father-son stories particularly captivate me—one in the New Testament, the other in the Old Testament, each with a very different outcome. The New Testament story tells of a young man who rebelled and the father who handled it well, patiently waiting for the son to come to his senses and return. That story ends with a grand display of mercy and grace as the wayward lad, expecting nothing more than a slave's place in the household, arrives home to see his dad bounding across the field to embrace him. A robe, a ring, a feast, and best of all, a restored relationship. The father cries, "This son of mine was dead and has come to life again; he was lost and has been found" (Luke 15:24). Everybody loves that story!

THE REBEL PRINCE CHARMING

The Old Testament story isn't anybody's favorite. It has a sad, disappointing ending. This father is a national hero, a mighty king. He has a boy who goes bad—more than one, actually—and he owns a great deal of responsibility for the sins of his son.

The king is David, of course. A great man of God, Israel's greatest leader, something of a Renaissance man before his time. As a teenager, he faced a giant on the battlefield with nothing but a sling and a stone and his rock-solid faith in the Lord. As a result, King Saul invited him to serve in his court as a poet and musician, which he did faithfully until the king turned on him and tried to murder him in a jealous rage. Though the Lord had rejected Saul because of his disobedience and had anointed David to replace him, David was forced to live the life of a fugitive for a dozen years or more. He survived, by the grace of God, and began his reign soon after Saul died.

At the age of thirty, David began to build his nation's power and prosperity, growth that continued without interruption for forty years. One quaint historian said that during David's reign there was "a chicken in every pot and a grape on every vine." The boundaries stretched, the economy boomed, the people's hearts turned again to their God, and the Lord found in this king a man after His own heart. But his children would tell another story . . . especially Absalom. Inside the palace walls, Absalom's world was "a perfect pandemonium of suspicion, and intrigue, and jealousy, and hatred—all breaking out, now into incest and now into murder."[1]

On the one hand, we don't want to be too hard on David, because his devotion and faithfulness to the Lord would put many of us to shame. On the other hand, we don't want to place him on a pedestal or idolize him as a spiritual superhuman. While he was Israel's greatest king up until the birth of Christ, idealized by Jews past and present, he suffered from the same disease of sin that afflicts you and me. The nation venerated him as a hero, but Amnon, Tamar, Adonijah, Absalom, and dozens of other children could have told another story. To them, he was Dad, which means they saw him when no one else was looking. Their view wasn't at all flattering.

As we examined David's private world in the previous chapter, we saw a privately flawed man, a passive father. When Absalom came to terms with the fact that David would not vindicate Tamar and hold her rapist brother accountable, he determined to make justice his responsibility. According to Deuteronomy 22:25–26 and Leviticus 20:17, Amnon was in double jeopardy for rape and incest. He deserved banishment at the very least, though execution would have been appropriate. At least a trial would have cleared Tamar of any wrongdoing so that marriage and some semblance of a normal life could be hers. David did nothing. The result of the king's inactivity: Absalom's resentment slowly festered into seething rebellion.

This particular story explores the rebellion of a son. Obviously, girls can and do rebel. However, it is a fact that a boy's rebellion is usually more aggressive in nature, much more overt. Girls often rebel in self-destructive ways that usually don't involve breaking the law or contributing to social statistics. Their anger tends to turn inward and mask itself in other ways, including anorexia, self-mutilation, codependency, and promiscuity. Boys, in contrast, tend to turn their anger on others. According to James Dobson's book *Bringing Up Boys*:

> Boys, when compared to girls, are six times more likely to have learning disabilities, three times more likely to be registered drug addicts, and four times more likely to be diagnosed as emotionally disturbed. They are at greater risk for . . . all forms of antisocial and criminal behavior. . . . 77 percent of delinquency-related court cases involve males. . . . Ninety percent of those in drug treatment programs are boys. Ninety-five percent of kids involved in juvenile court are boys.
>
> Perhaps the most disturbing evidence of the crisis has involved the increase in violence among males, especially the terrifying school shootings in Littleton, Colorado; Jonesboro, Arkansas; Springfield, Oregon; Paducah, Kentucky; Gibson, Oklahoma; Santee and El Cajon, California . . . . Most of the young killers to this point have been young white males who couldn't explain their motives. When asked why, most simply said, "I don't know."[2]

KEEPING TRUTH AT A DISTANCE

Absalom would have had no trouble pinpointing his reasons. By the time of the events described in 2 Samuel 14, Absalom had been living with his maternal grandfather in Geshur, fewer than one hundred miles north of Jerusalem. Though David secretly longed to reconcile with Absalom, he remained passive concerning their relationship. After three years of inexplicable silence, Joab gave the king a nudge in the right direction.

Joab was David's chief commander on the battlefield. He had been with David from the beginning and, for decades, served the king with unquestioned loyalty. In fact, when David wanted Uriah, Bathsheba's husband, killed in battle, Joab was the man who received the note and carried out those fatal orders without hesitation or question. He was three parts rottweiler and the rest pit bull, a military and political animal to the bone. Because Joab was not particularly known for his sentimentality, we can only guess that having Absalom back in Jerusalem was good for David's career. By way of an elaborate scheme, he convinced David that bringing Absalom back from exile was wise.

> Then the king said to Joab, "Behold now, I will surely do this thing; go therefore, bring back the young man Absalom." Joab fell on his face to the ground, prostrated himself and blessed the king; then Joab said, "Today your servant knows that I have found favor in your sight, O my lord, the king, in that the king has performed the request of his servant." So Joab arose and went to Geshur and brought Absalom to Jerusalem. However . . . (2 Samuel 14:21–24)

"However . . ." Such a powerful word. It has the unique power to render everything preceding it pointless. David agreed that Absalom should come home, but . . .

"However the king said, 'Let him turn to his own house, and

let him not see my face.' So Absalom turned to his own house and did not see the king's face" (2 Samuel 14:24).

If you ever have the chance to visit the Holy Land, take some time to walk around the boundary of the old city. It won't take you very long because ancient Jerusalem was remarkably small. Very little distance separated their houses, and the relatively small space would have required David and Absalom to work at avoiding contact. What kind of welcome home was *this*? What was David trying to avoid: his son or the truth of his own failings as a father?

I have found John White's *Parents in Pain* to be a penetrating, sometimes uncomfortable book to read. He writes with great empathy for parents of wayward children, but he insists that healing estranged relationships requires that we bravely embrace the truth—especially if it happens to be difficult.

At one point I wondered whether to deal with the different kinds of trouble children get into: drugs, alcohol, crime, homosexuality, secret marriages, pregnancy/paternity and so on. Yet I realized that in one sense it makes little difference what the nature of the problem is. Parental reactions run along the same lines. Shock is shock. Mistrust is mistrust. Rage is rage, weariness is weariness and despair, despair. Whatever the cause of our struggles, our human reactions follow similar patterns. And it is these you need help with. I want to give you a hand in getting up off the floor to live, even to experience joy again.

My goal is higher still. . . . I would like to open a door

for you, a door of hope . . . through which you may enter a fuller and richer life than you could have known before. For the God I believe in specializes in bringing good out of evil, strength out of pain and joy out of tragedy.

The goodness begins when you face the truth squarely, however much it sickens you. As much as you want to walk away and live someplace else, you did marry. You did produce children. They are alive and they are yours. The problem won't go away by pretending they are not there.

The problems include your feelings—your hurt, your rage, your panic, your disappointment, your shame, your humiliation, your alternate wish to yell at someone (your spouse, your child, your child's friends, the schoolteacher) and to lock yourself in the bathroom and talk to nobody. Look at them all. They exist. They are part of the problem you face. Even the sense of despair. And to look at them, to be able to face them fully and honestly, and to size them up is the first step in solving them. You cannot solve problems you close your eyes to.[3]

Some of you reading this book are doing what David did. He kept his estranged son in close proximity but refused to look at him, restore the relationship, or examine himself. Perhaps you have been dodging some painful realities. You know the wrong that stands between you and that other person. You know you're responsible for some, if not all of it, yet you choose to pretend it doesn't exist. The details of the relational train wreck feel as though they will overwhelm you with feelings and perspectives you cannot bear. Unfortunately, the solution you have chosen will not work forever. Silence solves nothing. The longer you wait, the greater the distance grows. So . . . you understand that father-son standoff.

"Now Absalom lived two full years in Jerusalem, and did not see the king's face" (2 Samuel 14:28).

Bear in mind that Absalom had children—two sons and a daughter, whom he named Tamar after his sister. David's grandchildren lived within walking distance of his home, yet he did nothing to reconcile with his son, even for their sakes. Absalom desperately wanted to restore his relationship with his father. He left a comfortable life on his grandfather's estate, presumably enjoying the warmth and acceptance of that family, and took up residence in the tight community of Jerusalem, only to be ignored by his own father.

SCREAMING TO BE HEARD

After two years of awkward silence, Absalom contacted Joab hoping that he might be able to nudge David in the right direction again. Receiving no response, he tried again. Ignored a second time, Absalom decided to make his presence felt more keenly by torching the general's barley crop, which was not unlike killing a roach with a shotgun. It worked. "Then Joab arose, came to Absalom at his house and said to him, 'Why have your servants set my field on fire?'" (2 Samuel 14:31).

Let me briefly recap Absalom's experience to this point. He grew up with a father whose job it was to lead the nation with godliness and justice, yet all the while, David collected women for his harem against the Law of God. Absalom saw this weakness for women lead his father to commit adultery with his friend's wife and cover it up with murder. He witnessed his father dismiss the agony of Tamar as though it were nothing and ignore his repeated cries for justice for two full years, yet David wept and mourned when Amnon was killed. Absalom lived in exile for three years until David presumably summoned him home, to which he eagerly responded, only to be told, "I won't seek your life, but I don't want you around me." Finally weary of waiting and desperate for some kind of resolution, he sought the help of an intermediary, who proved to be just as unresponsive as the king. To get Joab's attention, Absalom had to burn his field.

Do you see what I see? I see a young man who patiently waits for his father to do what is right, only to be disappointed time after time after time. I see a son who has to scream to be heard. I see a childrearing process that models hypocrisy, rewards good behavior with neglect, and responds to a child's legitimate needs only when he does something horribly wrong. I see years of justifiable anger building toward critical mass—a ticking time bomb beneath the palace.

I in no way excuse Absalom's response to the terrible events in his life. He had other choices to make. He could have returned to Geshur to live in peace with his grandfather. But let's be honest, David bears a great deal of the responsibility for Absalom's explosion. Seven years after Tamar's rape, five years after Amnon's murder, when David finally agreed to see his son face to face, his passive behavior lit Absalom's fuse.

> So when Joab came to the king and told him, he called for
> Absalom. Thus he came to the king and prostrated himself
> on his face to the ground before the king, and the king
> kissed Absalom. (2 Samuel 14:33)

A kiss in the ancient Near Eastern culture was much like our handshake. David gave him the customary gracious greeting, which was also a symbol of kinship, but nothing more. This was a time for more than a kiss, even a heartfelt one. This was a time for words—actually, a very long talk. How much better it would have been for David to pull Absalom to his feet and embrace him with the words, "Absalom, Absalom, come here. I can't tell you how many nights I've laid awake realizing all the things I did wrong. I can't fully express the anguish of my soul when I recall how I have neglected you, how absent I have been. How wrong I have been! Absalom, please forgive me." We see none of that. Just . . . a kiss.

Children will never stop seeking the love of their parents until their parents prove that it cannot be had. David's superficial kiss confirmed what Absalom had suspected.

FROM RESENTMENT TO REBELLION

The subsequent chapter in 2 Samuel begins with the words, "It came about after this . . ." After what? After the passive years. After the distance. After moving into the same city. After two more years of deafening silence. After seven nightmarish years following the rape. After hoping and praying for reconciliation. After a pathetic kiss.

"After this," Absalom obtained a chariot and gathered a band of loyal troops. He then stationed himself by the gate where people on their way to obtain justice from David would pass. He began to usurp David's authority, intercepting his citizens with the words, "See, your claims are good and right, but no man listens to you on the part of the king" (2 Samuel 15:3). Apparently, David's passivity extended to his public life, which gave Absalom ample opportunity to build loyalty among the people.

I didn't mention it before, but Absalom was not only a prince, but a handsome prince. His face and body had no blemishes or scars, and his long, flowing, black hair gave him film star good looks. For months on end, this striking figure dealt compassionately with people needing justice. Perhaps the scandals in the palace eroded the confidence of David's followers, which made the handsome prince even more attractive . . . and deceptive.

> Moreover, Absalom would say, "Oh that one would appoint me judge in the land, then every man who has any suit or cause could come to me and I would give him justice." And when a man came near to prostrate himself before him, he would put out his hand and take hold of him and kiss him. In this manner Absalom dealt with all Israel who came to the king for judgment; so Absalom stole away the hearts of the men of Israel. (2 Samuel 15:4–6)

Let me add a word of advice to anyone who serves as an associate to a leader. As long as you are associated with that leader, loyalty is job one. If you can't remain loyal to your leader, resign your position. Note that I didn't say you always have to agree. Loyalty doesn't mean you always agree. However, even in your disagreements, act in the best interest of your leader. If you can't do that, it's time to move on.

Absalom's duty as David's son was to persevere in the pursuit of a reconciled relationship, or at least retreat in dignified silence. Instead, he used his position to weaken and overthrow his father's leadership. Rather than win his father's heart, he decided to take his throne. In time, Absalom's scheme began to pay off.

> And the conspiracy was strong, for the people increased continually with Absalom.
>
> Then a messenger came to David, saying, "The hearts of the men of Israel are with Absalom." David said to all his servants who were with him at Jerusalem, "Arise and let us flee, for otherwise none of us will escape from Absalom. Go in haste, or he will overtake us quickly and bring down calamity on us and strike the city with the edge of the sword." (2 Samuel 15:12–14)

Rather than trying to reason with Absalom, David reacted with fear, and with good reason at this point. When resentment grows into rebellion, almost anything is possible, even murder. David, perhaps for the first time, recognized how deeply Absalom had been affected, and the king knew his own life was now in danger.

So the king went out and all his household with him. But
the king left ten concubines to keep the house. The king
went out and all the people with him, and they stopped at
the last house. (2 Samuel 15:16–17)

"The last house" most likely means the last residence in the
city before crossing the Kidron Valley, which runs between
Jerusalem and the Mount of Olives. I can see David stopping for
one last look at the city before leaving, perhaps forever. I imagine
the unvarnished truth about how he came to be exiled by his own
son came into clear focus. We see a different David after this
moment. No more passivity, no more pride, only vulnerability.
His heart had become contrite for his wrongdoing and grew
increasingly more tender toward Absalom. And when some
people threw rocks and spit on him, he restrained his friends
from retaliating and accepted the abuse.

David's retreat from Jerusalem took him to the very bottom.
In this excruciating, lonely place in life, pride and spite fall away,
leaving only a willingness to accept humiliation for wrongdoing.
It is in this moment that we see David's true greatness. When
afflicted, most people turn bitter; his spirit only grew sweeter.
Seeing him crushed this way brought out the best in his loyal
followers. In characteristic eloquence, F. B. Meyer writes:

The bitter hour of trial revealed a love on the part of his
adherents to which the old king may have become a little
oblivious. . . . His people tell him that he must not enter

127

the battle, because his life is priceless, and worth ten thousand of theirs.

It was as though God stooped over that stricken soul, and as the blows of the rod cut long furrows in the sufferer's back, the balm of Gilead was poured into the gaping wounds. Voices spoke more gently; hands touched his more softly. . . . Compassion rained tender reassurances about his path; and, better than all, the bright-harnessed angels of God. . . . God's protection encamped about his path and his lying-down.[4]

We don't know how long the rebellion lasted. What we do know is how extreme Absalom's hatred had become. Ahithophel had been a friend and adviser to the king until Absalom moved into the palace. Then he became Absalom's best friend . . . and wicked adviser.

Ahithophel said to Absalom, "Go in to your father's concubines, whom he has left to keep the house; then all Israel will hear that you have made yourself odious to your father. The hands of all who are with you will also be strengthened." So they pitched a tent for Absalom on the roof, and Absalom went in to his father's concubines in the sight of all Israel. (2 Samuel 16:21–22)

Note the location of Absalom's power play: the roof of the palace. We can't help but wonder if it was on the very spot where David first lusted for Bathsheba.

David made no attempt to retaliate. In fact, the whole matter broke and softened his heart. Eventually, the civil war turned to favor David's loyal troops, who had Absalom's army on the run. When David received the news, he showed great mercy as he issued strict orders to spare his son's life.

> The king charged Joab and Abishai and Ittai, saying, "Deal gently for my sake with the young man Absalom." And all the people heard when the king charged all the commanders concerning Absalom. . . . "Protect for me the young man Absalom!" (2 Samuel 18:5, 12)

Unfortunately, David's normally loyal commander, Joab, disobeyed the order.

> Now Absalom happened to meet the servants of David. For Absalom was riding on his mule, and the mule went under the thick branches of a great oak. And his head caught fast in the oak, so he was left hanging between heaven and earth, while the mule that was under him kept going. When a certain man saw it, he told Joab and said, "Behold, I saw Absalom hanging in an oak." (2 Samuel 18:9–10)

When the crusty, war-hardened general heard the news, he scolded the messenger for failing to kill Absalom on the spot. Then Joab, ornery as a junkyard dog, gathered a small squad and set out for Absalom's tree with murder in mind.

Then Joab said, "I will not waste time here with you." So he took three spears in his hand and thrust them through the heart of Absalom while he was yet alive in the midst of the oak. And ten young men who carried Joab's armor gathered around and struck Absalom and killed him. (2 Samuel 18:14–15)

Joab clearly disobeyed the order of his king, probably for the first time. He was as mean and as ruthless as they come, but he was practical to a fault. He had the leader of the rebellion in his sights and he knew that killing Absalom would bring a swift end to the civil war, which would restore David's kingdom and spare the lives of his countrymen on both sides. He also knew that David would not have the heart to make this very difficult decision. If Absalom remained alive, his forces would have continued the fight. As it happened, the rebel army quickly broke ranks and scattered. Content that the war was over, Joab restrained his army and let the people go home in peace.

When Joab's messengers arrived with news from the field, not surprisingly, David's first question was about neither the battle nor the soldiers, but about Absalom.

Then the king said to the Cushite, "Is it well with the young man Absalom?" And the Cushite answered, "Let the enemies of my lord the king, and all who rise up against you for evil, be as that young man!" (2 Samuel 18:32)

That's a gentle, archaic Hebrew way of saying, *Absalom is*

dead. The Hebrew text says that David "shook" in response to the news. The loss of yet another son by tragic circumstances was more than he could bear, especially after having come to terms with the part he played in his downfall. And worst of all, any possibility for reconciliation vanished with Absalom's death.

> The king was deeply moved and went up to the chamber over the gate and wept. And thus he said as he walked, "O my son Absalom, my son, my son Absalom! Would I had died instead of you, O Absalom, my son, my son!" (2 Samuel 18:33)

Those are the achingly sorrowful words of a dad grieving the loss of a son with whom he had many unresolved issues. Few words in all the Old Testament are more tragic than these.

TURNING FROM RESENTMENT TO RECONCILIATION

Anger doesn't become resentment overnight; it's a process that takes time. So does repairing a relationship. Reconciliation rarely occurs suddenly and completely. Usually, it begins with a breakthrough and then grows as the two people learn to trust each other again. Typically, the longer the estrangement, the longer the time for complete restoration.

THREE VALUABLE PRINCIPLES

As you think of that family member—a child, a parent, a sibling—and you seek to repair the breach in your relationship, keep three exceedingly important principles in mind.

131

First, *fractured relationships begin to heal when we're willing to hear and admit the truth*. Relationships are built upon truth, even when that truth is unpleasant. Division occurs when we first fail to listen to the other. This breakdown in communication allows us to shield ourselves from accountability and behave in ways that further alienate the person we claim to love. If you find yourself doing most of the talking in a relationship, reluctant to hear everything the other has to say, you are likely the one more in the wrong. How valuable is that person to you? How significant is your relationship?

Even if it's been years, I plead with you to hear that person and admit the truth about yourself . . . whatever it is and wherever it leads. It will likely be an awkward and humiliating conversation, painful and tearful. You may have to allow the anger of your loved one to be fully expressed as you accept responsibility for a number of failures. This is the time you must ask which you value more: your pride or your loved one?

The fracture in your relationship will never find complete healing until you are willing to hear and admit the truth. I hardly need to tell you that failing to reconcile that relationship will haunt and damage you, if not destroy you, in the long run. And let me assure you, lingering family conflicts can be the most damaging.

Second, *reconciliation continues to occur as we quit controlling and manipulating the other person*. When we control or manipulate the interaction between ourselves and the other, we shut down communication, which effectively puts the relationship on hold. If you're manipulating, you're not relating. This can occur in a number of different ways, but the most common in the midst of conflict is blame. One author wisely writes,

> Whenever we place blame, we are looking for a scapegoat for a real dislocation in which we ourselves are implicated. Blame is a defensive substitute for an honest examination of life that seeks personal growth in failure and self-knowledge in mistakes.[5]

This does not mean we cannot air our grievances with another person. Communication and blame have very different motives. Communication is the process of understanding and being understood. Blame, on the other hand, is something we primarily do within our own minds. It seeks to lay responsibility for the sorry state of things on the other person, all without the need for talking. By our attitude, we declare, *I don't need truth. I don't need to hear from the other person. I know what happened and it's all his or her fault.*

When we control or manipulate the relationship, whether by blame or some other means, we remove God as the mediator. That puts us in charge—a very dangerous position for everyone.

Third, *final relief comes when we release all resentment and accept our responsibility.* After I spoke on this topic, a young woman said to me, "I am a daughter with a relationship with my parents just like what you described. What can I do now to make my folks listen?"

I said, "Well, nothing. That's God's job. Ruth Graham once

said, 'It's my job to love Billy; it's God's job to make him good.' It's your job to own your part of the conflict, whatever it is. Focus your energy on taking responsibility for yourself, and allow God to change the other person's heart."

And here's the hard part: what if the other person's heart *never* changes? This happens all the time. It might happen to you. This doesn't change the principle. If you fail to release your resentment and take ownership of your responsibility, you will remain trapped. You will have exchanged joy for a mediocre life—and for what? The illusion of being right.

The other person might have died before you were able to reconcile. You may need to visit the gravesite, stand or kneel in prayer, and ask God to bring you inner peace. You may need a counselor to help you pull up the anchor of resentment and clean off the debris as you bring yourself back on course. Whatever your circumstance, don't delay. Don't waste another day wrestling with yourself. Release your long-standing resentment. Quit trying to be responsible for making the other person do what is right. Take responsibility for yourself.

⁓

I am grateful to our Savior, Jesus Christ, for making "wrong" such a safe thing to be. He paid the penalty for every wrong we could do—every foul thought, every ugly action, every impure motive, every retaliatory moment—leaving us nothing to pay. He covered every transgression by shedding His blood on the cross. If you have accepted His free gift of eternal life, you have the freedom and the power to accept responsibility for your own faults. No one can stand in condemnation of you: not your loved ones, not your enemies, not even Satan.

Truth be told, you have no excuse for leaving fractured, eroding relationships unhealed. You have nothing to lose but your pride. And what has that gotten you so far, anyway?

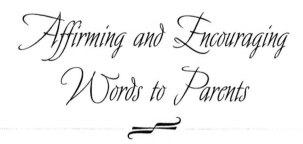

SEVEN

Affirming and Encouraging Words to Parents

A man in Phoenix, advanced in years and feeling ornery, picked up the telephone and called his son in New York. "I hate to ruin your day, but I have to tell you, your mother and I are getting a divorce. Neither on of us can go on together. Forty-five years of this misery is enough."

"Dad, what are you talking about?" His son sounded crushed.

"We can't stand the sight of each other any longer. And besides, you and your sister are adults now, so there's no reason for us to stay together. Matter of fact, I'm tired of talking about it, so you can tell your sister in Chicago for me." With that, he abruptly hung up.

Frantic, the son called his sister, who immediately flew into a fury. "There is no *way* they're getting a divorce!" she shouted. "I'll take care of this."

She called Phoenix and before her dad could finish *hello*, she tore into him. "You two are *not* going to throw away forty-five years of marriage just like that. You are *not* getting a divorce. Don't do a single thing until I get there. I'm calling my brother back and we'll both be there tomorrow. Until then, don't do a thing, YOU HEAR ME?" Without waiting for an answer, she slammed the phone down.

The old rascal hung up the phone, turned to his wife, and said with a smile, "Well, both of them will be here for Thanksgiving and they're paying their own way."

Some parents have a knack for driving their children crazy. Most others are quietly heroic. I recently saw a video clip of a poignant homecoming. A military transport plane had landed, and the family members of these returning warriors had gathered near the landing strip to see their loved ones at long last. The line of soldiers, all dressed in camouflage and lugging their gear, walked down the ramp.

One photographer had the presence of mind to turn his camera from the plane to the crowd of people, which included one particular woman—a wife, a mother—with a child on each side and one on her shoulders. The little boy on her shoulders held a sign that read, "My dad is my hero."

I lingered over that scene for a while. As I blinked away the tears, I imagined how her husband smothered the woman of his life with kisses, then picked up each child for a giant, long hug. I wondered what the little boy must have been thinking. As young as he was, probably nothing more than, *I love my dad, my hero.*

Merriam-Webster's Collegiate Dictionary defines *hero* as, "[One] admired for his achievements and noble qualities, one who shows great courage, an object of extreme admiration and devotion."[1] On behalf of your children who have never used the word—and possibly never will—you are their heroes, Mom and Dad. Despite how ordinary or how inadequate you feel, you are a person of great courage, possessing noble qualities, someone working to achieve something great: turning children into healthy adults. You are to be commended for taking on this terribly difficult and largely thankless task.

Oh, you're not perfect, and no one expects perfection but you. Certainly, you've made your mistakes, though the majority of your decisions have been sacrificial. You have poured yourself into your children, which sometimes leaves you empty. But let me assure you that your investment is not made in vain. Parenting is not an easy job and you don't get a lot of verbal affirmation. If you haven't heard this in a while, let me thank you on their behalf.

Thank you for the many sacrifices you make. Thank you for doing what is right even when things don't work out well. Thank you for saying what may be difficult for your children to accept and for being the truth teller when you'd rather be a pal. Thank you for loving them when you feel so unloved. Thank you for fulfilling your role with such devotion and faithfulness, even when you've run out of hope, energy, and ideas.

Thank you for the great service you do for all of us in the body, not just your children.

THE MODEL PARENT

In the last couple of chapters, we examined the family life of a great man who, despite his many impressive qualities, quit his role as father. In fact, I find little evidence in Scripture to suggest that David ever accepted responsibility for rearing any of his children. Amnon and Absalom were difficult sons, to be sure, but their father's passivity mixed with absence did little to curb their evil bents, leaving them no boundaries, little guidance, and few reasons to act better than their worst impulses.

I now want us to study the example of another father, one whose sons were also very difficult. He models a type of godly parenting that stops short of manipulation and control (which never yield good results in children) yet still manages to offer strong, loving guidance. He refused to indulge or ignore the poor behavior of his sons, yet he took appropriate responsibility as their father as he sought their highest and best good.

This father is the central character in one of the most familiar and best loved stories in the Bible. Strictly speaking, he's fictional, an imaginary character in a parable of Jesus. Yet he's also the most real father of all. In telling the story often called "The Prodigal Son" in Luke 15:11–32, Jesus revealed the parenting skills of his own Father. And by His example, we learn how a godly parent guides a child, however stubborn, rebellious, angry, or selfish he or she might be.

The main characters consist of a father and two rebel sons. The younger ran wild and everyone knew about it. The older son seethed in his self-righteous anger while everyone saw a loyal, obedient young man. (We will examine him in the next chapter.) Despite the poor character and stupid choices of his sons, I must point out that the father did nothing wrong by either of them. Both sons were guilty of rebellion, each in his own way, and somehow managed to make their father the scapegoat. Many parents can identify with this man's loneliness.

Ernest Shackleton, in his excellent book *The Voyage of the Endurance*, writes, "Loneliness is the penalty of leadership."[2] That's certainly true of parenting. When I think of the prodigal son's father, I see a lonely man in a lonely struggle. After all he had done for his boy, his son tossed him aside and opted for a long estrangement. After all he had hoped for, he lived with the very real possibility that he may never see his son again.

THE QUALITIES OF AN IDEAL PARENT

Looking at this story as a son, a father, and a grandfather, three broad observations come to mind.

First, *I notice that the father created a comfortable, nurturing, grace-filled environment.* This is one of the most important contributions a parent can make in a child's life. Words and actions are important, but the atmosphere we create has a huge impact on a child's sense of security and well-being. Jesus's description tells us that this father is no superhuman figure; he's just an ordinary man who loves his boys, loves their mother, and takes good care of his home and everyone in it.

Second, *Jesus described a man who was approachable and gracious.* The son apparently felt the freedom to speak his mind without fear of rebuke or rejection. The father didn't even fight his boy's terse demand. "Father, I want right now what's coming to me" (Luke 15:12 MSG). I see in the boy an impudence, a spirit of entitlement, a self-centered lack of respect for the fact that the wealth was his father's to release, not his to demand. Nevertheless, he stretched out his palm and said, in effect, "I want what's coming to me . . . and I want it *now.*"

According to Jewish law, recorded in Deuteronomy 21, a father was to distribute the family wealth evenly between his sons, with the eldest receiving double the amount of the others as "the right of the firstborn." In this case, the older son was to receive two-thirds of the father's estate, with the younger receiving one-third. Normally, of course, this was done upon the father's death, unless he chose to bequeath his fortune early. The son's request was crass; however, the father did receive a benefit—one we might be wise to consider. He chose to transfer his wealth to his children *before* he died, which means he was around to see them enjoy it and could rejoice along with them.

Third, *the dad knows his son.* Being older and wiser, he knows that tough times are inevitable. He knows that the boy is old enough to leave home, but he also knows that he's not mature enough to handle the temptations and demands of living on his own. He faced the challenge of this son coming to him with his self-centered hand held out, knowing, deep down, that everything would one day backfire. Nevertheless, this father offered no resistance. Because he knew that his son was not in a listening frame of mind, trying to impart wisdom would have proven pointless. Good parents know their children.

Families often come to this difficult moment of truth. For a variety of reasons, a child decides it's time to move out or away. As difficult as it feels, usually it's best to let him or her go. Meet the request with a good-faith effort to accommodate the move. I'm not suggesting that a parent should appear to call the child's bluff. Very often, it's not a bluff. I am suggesting that resisting a child's desire to leave the home will only obscure one problem with another. As long as he or she feels trapped, no one—least of all the child—will be able to acknowledge and address the real issues.

This father knew that a looser grip was his only hope of one day redeeming his son. I'm sure he also understood that the days ahead would grow much darker before his son would see the light. And he realized that such a day might never come.

THE ATTITUDES OF AN IDEAL PARENT

Though the story has been given the title "The Prodigal Son," the central figure in the story is the father. We identify with the wandering, returning son, but Jesus told the story to teach us about the Father. Luke 15 opens with the story of the lost sheep, in which we discover that the Father rejoices at the restoration of one sheep. His next story makes the same point using a recovered coin. In Luke 15:11–32, Jesus gives us a more detailed glimpse into the character of the Father, and in Him I find four outstanding parental attitudes worth emulating.

He Is Willing to Listen and to Risk

The father wasn't *obligated* to listen; he *chose* to listen. And he certainly didn't have to *hand over* his wealth; he chose to *release* it.

> There was once a man who had two sons. The younger said to his father, "Father, I want right now what's coming to me."
>
> So the father divided the property between them. It wasn't long before the younger son packed his bags and left

for a distant country. There, undisciplined and dissipated, he wasted everything he had. (Luke 15:11–13 MSG)

We are not told anything about the discussions that took place during the process. The father would have had to sell at least one-third of his entire estate in order to hand his son the cash, which would have taken time. We're told "it wasn't long before" the son left his home. Certainly, this father would have used that time to his advantage with at least one good father-son talk, perhaps several. I imagine he might have said something like this:

> Son, you've now got more money than you've ever had in your life. For the first time you will not only be living away from home, which you've never done before, but you'll be living without any accountability, boundaries, or influence from your family. I won't be around to ask the hard questions or to advise you.
>
> The world is a harsh place. There are street-smart people out there ready to take you for everything you've got. Be careful. Watch your money. Choose your friends very carefully. Most importantly, guard your heart. The principles I've taught you will work just as well away from me as they have during our time together. You'll soon be all on your own. A lot of fair-weather friends, once they discover you've got money, will plan to live off your cash. Don't let that happen.

Furthermore, you are sure to face temptations you never knew existed. Be strong. Walk wisely. Pure. Maintain a close walk with God.

You know the speech. It's the one that good parents give when their son or daughter goes off to college or boards the plane for boot camp or moves into an apartment with a few friends. Any parent willing to release a child must be willing to listen and to risk. This father gives his son the money he has coming.

He Is Willing to Release Him Completely

We see no resistance on the part of the father. There was no arguing, no pleading, no weeping, no clinging. He released his son to live on his own without controlling or manipulating him. He simply let him go.

One morning, the boy packed his belongings and took off on "a journey into a distant country," into unfamiliar geography and customs, an unknown culture having unexpected surprises, including unusual "friends" waiting for him. It wasn't long before he failed to remember his father's advice as he began to engage in "loose living." ("The word signifies wild and disorderly rather than [merely] extravagant or voluptuous living."[3]) He squandered his estate in a reckless pleasure binge, spending money without care. He was free! He was on his own. And he soon found lots of companions willing to help him party. They could spot an easy mark, so they clung to him like parasites.

"After he had gone through all his money, there was a bad famine all through that country and he began to hurt" (Luke 15:14 MSG).

We have no idea how long the money held out against his foolish spending, but eventually it began to run out. He downsized from a Manhattan penthouse to a second-floor flat across the tracks in Booger Holler. He finally hit bottom when a famine struck the land. This would have been like going broke just before the stock market crash in 1929. Anyone who has been completely out of resources and truly hungry can identify with the young man's plight. Desperation mixed with depression and panic resulted in his reaching the low-water mark of his life.

> He signed on with a citizen there who assigned him to his fields to slop the pigs. He was so hungry he would have eaten the corncobs in the pig slop, but no one would give him any. (Luke 15:15–16 MSG)

A man in his predicament will consider doing anything to survive, including eating things he never would have otherwise imagined. The only job the young man could find was sloppin' hogs—how degrading an occupation for a Jew! And even then, it didn't pay enough to keep his stomach full. When you're so hungry you covet a pig's filthy meal, you're starving!

Sometimes when observing Scripture, it's important to notice what the author chose *not* to say. We have to be careful about what conclusions we draw from his deliberate omission, but most parents would wonder, *Where's the father?*

The boy's father was where he had always been. He wasn't on a search for his son. He didn't write letters of encouragement. He refused to beg the boy to return or offer to change the household if he'd only return or promise to be a better father. We see no evidence of guilt or angst on the part of the father, feeling like a failure, or blaming himself for his son's condition. It's quite natural for a parent to go there. *What did I do wrong? What should I have said that I didn't say? What did I say I shouldn't have said? How did I cause it?* But this father did none of that. In his reaction to the boy's return, we find an important clue.

"When he was still a long way off, his father saw him. His heart pounding, he ran out, embraced him, and kissed him" (Luke 15:20 MSG).

The father had his eyes on the horizon, perhaps studying it several times a day as the boy's name passed over his lips in prayer, longing to see him safe, aching to be with him. The boy's father wasn't present with him in the depravity of the pigsty, but he never, ever forgot his son in his private talks with God.

He Was Willing to Wait for God to Change His Son

Read the following words slowly and carefully. Enter into them.

He was so hungry he would have eaten the corncobs in the pig slop, but no one would give him any.

That brought him to his senses. He said, "All those

farmhands working for my father sit down to three meals a day, and here I am starving to death. I'm going back to my father. I'll say to him, Father, I've sinned against God, I've sinned before you; I don't deserve to be called your son. Take me on as a hired hand." He got right up and went home to his father.

When he was still a long way off, his father saw him. His heart pounding, he ran out, embraced him, and kissed him. (Luke 15:16–20 MSG)

Note that the father didn't try to rush the boy's transformation by some means of manipulation despite how much he wanted his son home. He was willing to wait patiently and allow God to change his son's heart.

This is so easy to write, yet so terribly hard to do. Watching one of your children hit bottom is one of the most painful experiences a parent can endure. But don't miss the last line of that first sentence: "but no one would give him any."

Once, after I spoke on this subject, a mother approached me in tears. She spoke with difficulty as she said, "On my son's sixteenth birthday he got his first job, bought his first car, took his first drugs, got hooked, and I didn't see him for twenty years." After serving two jail sentences, he faced a third. That's when he woke up. The mother added, "I never went after him, but I always kept a light on for him."

The father in Jesus's story had to leave his son to wallow in a pigsty with all the consequences. In a similar way, the mother had to leave her son in prison, all alone with his thoughts. As difficult as that is for a parent, that's the way it has to be or the prodigal and his senses will always remain strangers. Furthermore, a faithful parent never gives up, always leaves the light on, and keeps his or her heart's door unlocked in the hope that suffering will achieve its goal.

Years ago I read a line that I have never forgotten: "Pain plants the flag of reality in the fortress of a rebel heart." The boy was hurting. He shared a pen with pigs. His stomach screamed with hunger. His job was a mockery of everything he once considered sacred. His body was a filthy, soiled, stinking testament to his fall from ritual purity as a Jew. He could go no lower.

He hit bottom, exactly where he needed to be in order to "come to his senses." The literal Greek sentence reads, "he came to himself." The venerable Baptist scholar A. T. Robertson writes, "As if he had been far from himself as he was from home. As a matter of fact he had been away, out of his head, and now began to see things as they really were."[4]

So, finally, the prodigal son's heart was humbled and genuinely contrite. It is helpful to remember that a contrite heart makes no demands, has no expectations, and blames no one else. This attitude appears in his rehearsed speech to his father: "Father, I've sinned against God, I've sinned before you; I don't deserve to be called your son. Take me on as a hired hand" (Luke 15:18–19 MSG). The broken young man practiced and honed his speech all the way back home. He memorized the words, having rehearsed them again and again.

I love how the next line reads: "He got right up and went home to his father" (Luke 15:20 MSG). He didn't get up and return to his house, or to his bedroom, or to his friends, or to his wealth, or to his social standing. None of those drew him home. He came home to *his father*. He longed to be with his dad, to restore that relationship. Remember this: in Jesus's story, the father is a word portrait of God the Father. Our God patiently waits for us to come to our senses . . . to return to Him in whom we find everything we long for and need. Unfortunately, we stubbornly refuse to do so until we've exhausted all other options and finally come to realize that our trying to provide for ourselves is futile.

I love the way one insightful poet put it:

> Whom have we, Lord, but Thee,
> Soul-thirst to satisfy?
> Exhaustless spring!
> The water's free!
> All other streams are dry.[5]

He Was Willing to Accept, Forgive, and Restore

"He got right up and went home to his father. When he was still a long way off, his father saw him. His heart pounding, he ran out, embraced him, and kissed him" (Luke 15:20 MSG).

The boy wiped his palms and gave his lines a final run-through as his home appeared in the distance. His heart must have skipped a beat. His father saw him coming "a long way off." Isn't that great? Dad was sitting on the front porch, scrutinizing any silhouette that appeared in the distance. He sat watching for the distinctive gait of his son. He was willing to wait, but he was earnest in it! His joy knew no bounds the day he recognized his boy. Without a moment's hesitation, he bounded across the fields to embrace his son with love.

What a contrast to the welcome Absalom received! After a five-year estrangement, all David would consent to give his son was a cold, reluctant kiss—nothing he wouldn't have given any visiting dignitary. By contrast, look at the welcome the prodigal received. The verbs reveal his father's feelings.

His father *saw* him
and *felt* compassion for him
and *ran*
and *embraced* him
and *kissed* him.

The kid smelled like sour swine slop, but his father never noticed. He hugged and kissed him more than once. The Greek form of the verb "to kiss" has a prefix that indicates that the father kissed him "fervently," which most likely means again and again and again. Take special note of the absence of condemnation or condescension. He didn't say, "Well, it's about time!" or "I hope you learned your lesson!" or "You ought to be ashamed of yourself!" None of that. We see only a father grateful to have his son in his embrace again. He didn't care about being right or being vindicated or having his pride appeased. He was willing to accept his son, forgive his foolishness, and restore their relationship.

In fact, when the boy tried to apologize, his father wouldn't even let him finish his well-rehearsed speech. "The son started his speech: 'Father, I've sinned against God, I've sinned before you; I don't deserve to be called your son ever again'" (Luke 15:21 MSG).

The son had more to say. Remember the rest? He was ready to add, "Take me on as a hired hand," but before he could finish, his father called over his shoulder,

> Quick. Bring a clean set of clothes and dress him. Put the family ring on his finger and sandals on his feet. Then get a grain-fed heifer and roast it. We're going to feast! We're going to have a wonderful time! My son is here—given up for dead and now alive! Given up for lost and now found! (Luke 15:22–24 MSG)

The best robe in the house would have belonged to the father. The ring was likely the family signet, which functioned much like today's credit card, giving him the ability to purchase what he wished and to obligate the family to pay debts. Furthermore, servants, hired or otherwise, rarely had the privilege of wearing sandals. Servants put sandals on the feet of others. A popular song among slaves during a shameful period of American history was "All God's Children Got Shoes." Since slaves went barefoot, it was a luxury worthy of describing heaven.

Once the son had been restored to his previous place of respect in the family, his father involved the whole village in welcoming the boy home. A "fatted calf" was a choice specimen from the herd, specially prepared over a number of days before slaughter to be particularly succulent and tender. And a whole calf would have been enough to feed a small village. The father declared, "Kill the calf, build a fire, and invite the town. We're having a barbecue!" Why? "My son is here—given up for dead and now alive! Given up for lost and now found!" (Luke 15:24 MSG). And they celebrated and danced and sang.

A great, old hymn captures the Father's heart of grace with these words:

> Who is a pardoning God like Thee?
> Or who has grace so rich and free?[6]

If any quality of God sets Him apart from the gods of cults and false religions, it is grace. No other religion claims a god who freely and fully pardons its followers. Those who seek to appease idols always have to work and keep working, prove and keep proving, earn and keep earning to receive the love of their god, who even then may decide it's not enough. Not our heavenly Father! The boy was still caked with the stench and grime of the pigsty, still dripping the sweat of his long walk home as his father placed a clean linen robe on him—the robe he normally reserved for himself. The father accepted his son as he was, forgave him freely, and restored him completely. Then he danced.

That scene makes me smile and clap my hands. The music and dancing drowned out all the prodigal's guilt and shame.

THREE QUESTIONS FOR FAITHFUL PARENTS

I want to put three questions before you. I hope you'll slow down long enough to consider each of them. Don't merely read through this last section in a rush to the next chapter. If you do, you will have invested the time but missed the benefits.

Do You Have a Parent You Need to Thank?

I opened by offering a few affirming, encouraging words for parents, but they don't mean nearly as much from me as they would from you. If you haven't been a mom or dad for very long, you may not have had sufficient time to feel the sometimes overwhelming sense of inadequacy and guilt that accompanies parenting. The doubt can be debilitating as parents think of all the things they should have done that they didn't, all the mistakes they made, the wisdom that they gained too late, the regrets, too many to number. Parents tend to forget the successes. We overlook the security we provided, the messes we cleaned up, the sacrifices we made, the times you and I found so special that our parents never considered.

Your parents need to hear from you. Don't wait for a holiday to express your gratitude. Thank them now with a handwritten note, and resolve to do it often. "Thank you for the hundreds of things you did that I never knew about, the many sacrifices you made so quietly, so unselfishly. Thank you for providing such nutritious food and protective shelter; I never even knew how much our house payment was, and I never saw the grocery bill. And thank you for loving me in spite of my ignorance, my occasional outbursts of anger, my disrespect, and the many times I caused you pain. Thank you."

If you want to make a parent's day, thank him or her. I'm not sure which will feel better: the satisfaction or the relief.

Do You Have a Son or Daughter You Need to Release?

This isn't a question you wait until your daughter or son is eighteen to answer. This is a question you begin to face the day you send your child to kindergarten and each time he or she asks, "Can I . . . ?"

Releasing your child is something you mentally practice well in advance of the day he or she leaves for college, or the military, or a marriage, or a job. Releasing a child is an emotional discipline that must be practiced daily. Believe me, I know how difficult it is. He or she lacks the maturity to know about the world and how dangerous it can be for the naive. You see perils your child can't begin to comprehend. Furthermore, you're tired. The responsibilities you face are legion. You have enough to think about with the stress you have, not to mention the added worry of allowing your child to do something that involves potential harm. And it may even require your involvement, which demands more energy than you have to give.

Here is something Cynthia and I have done that may help. We decided, as our four kids were growing up, that we would always say yes unless it was absolutely essential to say no. If you do this with integrity, you'll be surprised (and perhaps a little dismayed!) to see how few times no is the appropriate response. You see, no is the easy answer. It requires no thought, no effort, no expense, no risk, no anxiety, no discussion, no trust, no growth, nothing. Furthermore, it's a sure way to build resentment into the relationship, which will likely turn into a perpetual game of tug-of-war, maybe even outright rebellion.

We found the benefits of being yes parents to be far more rewarding than we could have imagined. Yes is not only a positive response, but it's a faith answer. It requires that we trust the Lord to watch over our children. We have to trust Him to enable them to rise to meet the extra responsibility that freedom demands. A lot of grace is in that trust. Our children usually felt so honored by our trust that they worked doubly hard to avoid letting us down. Yes required a personal investment of time and effort and frequently involved money, which constantly stretched our own comfort zone. Yes forced us to look for growth in our children, which would have been easy to overlook otherwise, and almost without exception, they surprised us with their maturity. It also kept the communication lines open and active.

For your investment of faith, you will enjoy a relationship relatively free of rebellion. Your children will soon learn that a no is not your desire, but that circumstances beyond your control—on a few occasions—demand it. Furthermore, they'll accept no more easily because it's relatively rare, and they have learned to appreciate the reality of limitations. You will soon discover that the freedom you grant your children often translates into greater freedom for yourself.

Best of all, the day you launch your child into the world to stand on his or her own will be much easier to take. You will do so with greater confidence that your son or daughter is well prepared to balance freedom and responsibility because he or she has had lots of practice.

Do You Have a Prodigal Who Needs Forgiveness and Restoration?

If so, the future of your strained and awkward relationship is mostly out of your control. I say mostly because there are things you can do in addition to praying for your son's or daughter's return. I urge you to adopt the attitude of your heavenly Father toward all of His prodigals.

Be willing to surrender the entire matter to the Lord, which will free you from a lot of worry and allow you the freedom to release your child. Until he or she feels free from your hostility, your guilt, your expectations, or any other controlling attitudes, you will prolong the estrangement. Let me repeat these three words forcefully: *release your child.*

Be willing to wait for the Lord to change your child without your feeling the need to step in and hurry the process along. If your child is too distracted by your reproving, instructing voice, he or she will be too distracted to notice the heart surgery God wants to do within them. Making them *good* is God's great goal for all of us. To borrow a line from Ruth Graham, your job is to love your child; it's God's job to make him or her good. Wait for the Lord. Let it be. God wants your son or daughter good even more than *you* do!

Be willing to accept, forgive, and restore. God's most winsome quality is His grace. And for us to demonstrate grace this amazing is a God-sized undertaking. Can you accept your child if he or she comes home, fully repentant, still stinking of pigsty mud? Can you lay aside the rejection and a lot of shaming remarks and your own pain without expecting your child to make it up to you? Can you restore your child to his or her former place of honor in your heart and in your life? Of course a solid and sure foundation of trust will have to be restored over time. The inner bruises and deep heart wounds will need time to heal. But the crucial question is, are you willing to accept, forgive, and restore when you get that long-awaited phone call?

The proof of your willingness is demonstrated when you wash and press your finest robe, when you polish that ring, keep a nice pair of sandals by the door, and have the invitations ready to mail. All that's left is the sound of that voice spoken in a tone of deep, authentic repentance, saying, "I'm back. I love you . . . Can I come home?"

Practice your answer, starting now: *yes!*

EIGHT

Confronting the "Older Brother Attitudes"

The stories Jesus told never failed to connect with real-life issues. I don't think it's any coincidence that He set His story of the prodigal son in the context of family, for at least two reasons. First, His allegory addressed two kinds of people within the Jewish community—or the Jewish family, if you will—who lived in sharp contrast to one another. Second, anyone with brothers and/or sisters can appreciate the almost primal emotions involved in sibling conflict. Irritating behavior by someone outside the family may draw frustration, while the same actions by a family member can inspire deep resentment, even hatred. As parents, we can't afford to take lightly persistent negative attitudes or menacing resentments between siblings. So as we examine the "older brother attitudes" in Jesus's parable, it's best if we apply the principles we discover to the family.

Jesus told His story to expose the true nature of the Pharisees. They, along with their graceless attitudes, lurked everywhere Jesus went. Their legalism was relentless. By the way, that Pharisaic spirit lives on in many (most?) Christian circles. As one courageous author wrote:

There are people who do not want us to be free. They do not want us to be free before God, accepted just as we are by his grace. They don't want us to be free to express our faith originally and creatively in the world. They want to control us; they want to use us for their own purposes. They themselves refuse to live arduously and openly in faith, but huddle together with a few others and try to get a sense of approval by insisting that all look alike, talk alike, and act alike, thus validating one another's worth.

They try to enlarge their numbers only on the condition that new members act and talk and behave the way they do. These people infiltrate communities of faith "to spy out our freedom which we have in Christ Jesus" and not infrequently find ways to control, restrict and reduce the lives of free Christians. Without being aware of it we become anxious about what others will say about us, obsessively concerned about what others think we should do. We no longer live the good news but anxiously try to memorize and recite the script that someone else has assigned to us.[1]

Another place we find modern-day Pharisees, or "grace-killers" as I call them, is the family. The home is the last place many would look, though it is the first place legalism rears its ugly head.

Legalism in the home? Yes. Perhaps you never thought of the behavior of some family members that way before. Grace-killers have been around for a very long time and they are everywhere. For as long as there has been forgiveness, there have been those who prefer to hold grudges, condemn, and criticize. For as long as there has been the offer of freedom, there have been those who love to take away our liberty. For as long as we have been able to fly spiritually, there have been those who see it as their calling to clip our wings and push us down and hold us back. For as long as there have been prodigal sons and daughters who acknowledge and repent of their wrongdoing, there have been older brothers and sisters who have resented their return. And they resist any thought of fellowship, certainly in the deep sense of the word. Grace-killers don't just pollute churches with their conveniently chosen standards of worthiness; they suck the life out of an otherwise happy and wholesome home. The only thing that will release your family from the debilitating control of a legalist is truth. It has the power to set the unforgiving and condemning critics free—if only they will allow it. Unfortunately, they usually don't.

THE ANATOMY OF A PHARISEE

Return with me to the first century. Let's reenter a scene where Jesus is teaching a group of His followers.

> So Jesus was saying to those Jews who had believed Him, "If you continue in My word, then you are truly disciples of Mine; and you will know the truth, and the truth will make you free." (John 8:31–32)

Many people are familiar with the statement "the truth will make you free," but few are aware of Jesus's audience and the circumstance that prompted His words. He spoke them to new Jewish converts, former disciples of the Pharisees, who ruled their followers by severe condemnation and controlling intimidation. Brennan Manning describes the legalizers of Jesus's day particularly well.

> The Pharisees, who carried religion like a shield of self-justification and a sword of judgment, installed the cold demands of rule-ridden perfectionism because that approach gave them status and control, while reassuring believers that they were marching in lock-step on the road to salvation. The Pharisees falsified the image of God into an eternal, small-minded bookkeeper whose favor could be won only by the scrupulous observance of laws and regulations. Religion became a tool to intimidate and enslave rather than liberate and empower.[2]

The Pharisees knew the Torah, the first five books of the Old Testament Scriptures. But they didn't stop with studying the written Scriptures and committing much of it to memory; they added to it. In the spirit of obedience—a sincere spirit, I'm convinced—they tacked on not dozens, but hundreds of rules and regulations, instructions they believed to be on the same plane with the inspired words Moses wrote. They were so convinced by their own standards of worth before God, they were blinded to the underlying motives: status and control. If someone didn't fall in line with those rules and regulations, the Pharisees wrote him or her off as unworthy of God's special relationship with the Jewish family. Anyone who didn't measure up to this false righteousness lived a life of intimidation and fear as they existed under the thumb of these self-appointed judges. Until . . .

A maverick prophet from the northern countryside of Israel—a self-appointed "messiah," an unlettered nobody by pharisaical standards—began to travel around and preach to the general public. He was controversial in His views of righteousness and absolutely scandalous in His choice of disciples. The more popular He became, the more the legalists resented Him. This resentment only intensified as questionable individuals joined His band of disciples, like Matthew.

> After that He went out and noticed a tax collector named Levi sitting in the tax booth, and He said to him, "Follow Me." And he left everything behind, and got up and began to follow Him. (Luke 5:27–28)

Levi is the surname of the disciple we know as Matthew, the writer of the first book of our New Testament. At the time of Jesus's calling, he was a tax collector, a turncoat, a Jew who acted as a representative of the oppressive Roman Empire. His job was to take money from his countrymen, often under threat of imprisonment, in order to fill the war chest of Rome. As a side benefit, he received special treatment and the right to demand more than was owed so that he could fill his own wallet. If the tax were ten coins, he would present a bill for twelve and keep the difference. To better their own position, tax collectors betrayed their comrades, exchanging their Jewish solidarity to become the quisling puppets of Rome. Consequently, tax collectors were universally hated men, much like those Jews who cooperated with Hitler's persecution during the Nazi holocaust of the 1940s. Pharisees wouldn't as much as let the skirts of their robes touch a tax collector, to say nothing of treating them kindly or choosing them as disciples.

So the Galilean rabbi shocked the experts of the Law and the Pharisees by forgiving sins (something only God can do), then He called the worst of sinners to join His inner circle of twelve disciples (something no respectable teacher would do). Those decisions were enough to send the grace-killers into orbit, but it's what He did next that blew them out of the water.

> And Levi gave a big reception for Him in his house; and there was a great crowd of tax collectors and other people who were reclining at the table with them. (Luke 5:29)

Matthew "left everything behind, and got up and began to follow Him" (Luke 5:28). He was converted. A changed man. A believer. And to celebrate his new life, he threw a big reception for all his tax-collecting cronies and, according to Matthew's own Gospel, a whole houseful of other sinners and outcasts as well. Can you picture it? Jesus at a banquet table, surrounded by and enjoying being with every kind of person a Pharisee would shun as unworthy of association, unworthy of the Covenant, unworthy of God's favor.

Now, as you read this, I suspect you're feeling pretty safe. Maybe even a little smug. I'll admit it. I don't exactly appreciate the significance of dining with tax collectors either. I don't know any IRS agents personally, but I'm sure many of them are nice people. So let's put this in terms we can comprehend.

Imagine you are a member of a committee charged with the responsibility for finding a pastor to lead your congregation. You meet with a young man with a fine education, a good résumé, and references from people you don't know. His theology and personality appear to be a good match, so you schedule another meeting to allow other members of the church leadership to meet him. In the meantime, you discover that he frequents a part of town known for its raucous night life. In fact, he often goes to a gay bar, not to pass out tracts or wear a sandwich board with Bible verses painted on it, but to eat dinner. After eating, he enjoys playing pool or a few rounds of darts with the homosexual men who go there regularly. They know his name and he knows each of them. They are his friends. He doesn't condone their lifestyle, nor does he defend any sinful actions. He behaves himself, but he also spends some of his time there and he is being used by God to minister to them.

How does that strike you? Honestly.

Perhaps homosexuals don't give you any discomfort. Insert the demographic of your choice: skinheads, Republicans, liberals, Democrats, Catholics, another race, the very rich . . . you have a category. It's easy to look down our noses at the Pharisees for their false righteousness until our own private preferences and sensibilities have been trampled upon. Let's face it, we all have a little Pharisee in us.

Thankfully, Jesus did His Father's will and accepted the

invitation to attend a dinner party with this collection of Israel's most hated sinners. Surrounded by them, He enjoyed a fine meal, perhaps even music and laughter. Being surrounded by all of them, just think of the opportunity He had! The legendary Marine General "Chesty" Puller once said, "All right, they're on our left, they're on our right, they're in front of us, they're behind us . . . they can't get away this time."[3] Jesus sat for a whole evening surrounded by the very people He wanted to reach, people who would never approach God or His buildings or His representatives. Instead, God approached them in the person of Jesus Christ, who brought them the truth that would set them free.

Now notice who the Pharisees approached with their complaints:

> The Pharisees and their scribes began grumbling at His disciples, saying, "Why do you eat and drink with the tax collectors and sinners?" (Luke 5:30)

Isn't that like a Pharisee? They don't have the courage or integrity to address Jesus directly, so they grumble their complaints to His disciples. The Greek word is *egonggoodzon*, it sounds like what it is, a low-pitched, hushed tone. *Strong's Lexicon* defines it this way:

> 1) to murmur, mutter, grumble, say anything against in a low tone. 1a) of the cooing of doves. 1b) of those who confer secretly together. 1c) of those who discontentedly complain.[4]

That's how Pharisees of any era maintain their dominance. They deal in innuendo, guilt by association, whisper campaigns, and demagoguery. They focus on the darker aspects of human nature: suspicion and shame. "How can you follow a teacher who hangs around with *those* kind of people?"

Their tactics didn't escape Jesus's notice. They attacked in secret, but He answered openly. He had no reason to hide the truth.

> And Jesus answered and said to them, "It is not those who are well who need a physician, but those who are sick. I have not come to call the righteous but sinners to repentance." (Luke 5:31–32)

The truth of Jesus's message revolved around a word that no Pharisee had in his vocabulary: grace. How to become genuinely righteous, how to recover from sin, how to return home to the heavenly Father, how to find a purpose, a reason to go on after making a miserable mess of life. But to get there, we have to cross the grace bridge.

I recently found myself on the receiving end of grace. I was traveling down the road in my pickup at a fairly good clip and noticed the festive colors of blue and red flashing in my rearview mirror. My hope that the police officer was after the car in front of me proved to be false. After requesting my ID, he asked, "Do you know why I stopped you?"

"Yes sir," I stammered. (I use "sir" a lot when an officer of the law is standing at my window.)

"Do you know how fast you were going?"

I said, "No sir, I don't. Maybe my speedom—"

"Yeah, all speedometers are broken."

I'm just joking about that part. I readily admitted that I wasn't watching my speed and really had no excuse for going so fast. Then I heard those wonderful words of grace: "I'll let you off with a warning this time."

I felt relieved, elated, humbled, and grateful all at once. You know why? Because I didn't deserve to have my offense go unpunished. I deserved a speeding ticket. The police officer extended grace, undeserved merit. With grace, you don't receive what you deserve; you receive good things you haven't earned and cannot repay. And I should add, that officer's attitude of grace stayed with me. It not only filled my heart with gratitude, it made my right foot lighter.

To wrap up these thoughts on legalism, let me summarize by stating that Pharisees want justice. Jesus offers freedom. Pharisees expect disciples to earn the respect of their master before being taught. Jesus wants us to come to Him as we are. No one has to clean himself up in order for God to accept him or her as a sinner. Don't think you need to quit smoking or drinking, lay aside drugs, go straight, or undergo any other self-improvement project in hopes of earning God's favor. Grace relieves us of the need to "clean up." Remember Saul of Tarsus? While on his way to Damascus to get rid of Christians, he was converted to Christ. His getting "cleaned up" followed his conversion. Jesus attended tax-collector dinner parties for the same reason a physician goes to the hospital to do surgery. That's where He's needed.

THE STORY OF US

Now then, let's see how all this relates to Jesus's story. Very often the focus of attention in Jesus's parable of the prodigal son is the wasteful, ungrateful, foolish boy who squanders his inheritance and then comes crawling home. The story isn't called "The Faithful Father" or "The Self-Righteous Sibling," probably because we most identify with the prodigal. We like to think he is us. We can identify with his stupidity. And we long to know the joy of forgiveness and experience the opportunity to start over.

The younger brother had a great life to start with—a great dad, a secure living, a roof over his head, plenty to eat, servants to help him, cattle to raise, and, should his father die, one-third of the estate coming to him with none of the responsibilities of leadership that his brother would bear. He demanded his cash early and soon took off for a distant land with no boundaries and no accountability. His foolish choices landed him in poverty, fighting pigs for scraps of food. When he tired of the sores, the diarrhea, the cramps of starvation, the brown taste in his mouth, and the constant emptiness within, he came to his senses. Slavery in his father's house would be better than freedom among the swine, so he returned to his father expecting nothing.

When he arrived home, instead of rejection or chastisement, he received grace—a robe, a ring, a pair of shoes . . . and a giant welcome home party with the whole town. Why? Said the father, "This son of mine was dead and has come to life again; he was lost and has been found" (Luke 15:24). Soon the party was in full swing, with great food, joyous music, lots of singing and dancing, full of praise to God for the return of a beloved son. How delightful! Everything was perfect, except . . .

> [The father's] older son was in the field, and when he came and approached the house, he heard music and dancing. And he summoned one of the servants and began inquiring what these things could be. And he said to him, "Your brother has come, and your father has killed the fattened calf because he has received him back safe and sound." But he became angry and was not willing to go in. (Luke 15:25–28)

With the frowning face of a grace-killer, the legalist approached the camp to hear the sounds of a party he didn't throw for a brother. As a matter of fact, he never welcomed him home. These controllers not only withhold grace, but they resent anyone else who gives or receives it. The older brother remained sullen and distant, feeling self-righteously noble that he had been in the fields taking care of the family business while his shiftless brother was out wasting his life. His pride fueled the fire of his resentment.

His father came out and began pleading with him. But he answered and said to his father,

> Look! For so many years I have been serving you and I have never neglected a command of yours; and yet you have never given me a young goat, so that I might celebrate with my friends; but when this son of yours came, who has

devoured your wealth with prostitutes, you killed the fattened calf for him" (Luke 15:28–30)

We cannot help but be impressed by the father's grace. Most any other dad would have snatched that boy by the scruff of his neck and hauled him behind the woodshed for an attitude adjustment! Not this father. So full of grace, so patient. Despite his gentle reasoning, the self-righteous son clung to his resentment, something that Alcoholics Anonymous says is like drinking poison and expecting the other person to die. And from his point of view, he had good reason. With the prodigal wallowing in a pigsty, the older brother looked like a saint. Against his brother's waste and avarice, the legalist's own loyalty and conscientiousness looked superhuman. And with his rival off in a distant land, he could bask in the glow of his father's undivided attention.

"OLDER BROTHER ATTITUDES"

Look again at the older son's speech as I make a few observations.

First, *he was ungrateful.* He had obviously forgotten that he owned everything. Two-thirds of a sizable estate had passed to him. His father took an early retirement and left him in charge. Yet it wasn't enough unless his brother wound up having nothing.

Second, *he was petty and narcissistic.* His father had given him everything he owned, yet he resented his brother for receiving the honor of a welcome home celebration. "But I was the *good* son. Where's *my* party? Where's *my* reward?" Obviously he kept a detailed tally of every good deed and every righteous act.

It so fed his pride, he couldn't stand the "injustice" of grace.

Third, *he exaggerated his brother's sins in order to make his own righteousness shine brighter.* Note the detail he added to his brother's irresponsibility: "He has devoured your wealth *with prostitutes.*" The Greek expressions in this story don't suggest that the younger son had been overtly immoral. The term translated as "loose living" means "dissipation." The English word "prodigal" means "recklessly extravagant, characterized by wasteful expenditure, lavish."[5] One respected Greek dictionary reads, "Lk. 15.13 speaks of the dissipated life of the Prodigal without specifying the nature of this life. . . . It is simply depicted as carefree and spendthrift in contrast to the approaching [famine].[6] In other words, we are not told how he blew his fortune, only that it was done because he was foolish.

Fourth, *he had a lurid imagination.* Prostitutes? Why that particular sin? Perhaps the older son was more transparent in his ranting than he intended. Maybe if he had cashed in his inheritance and moved beyond the borders of accountability, he would have indulged himself and satisfied his sexual appetites.

Last, and most significant, *he felt that his relationship with his father depended upon his being faithful and good.* Read the passage again. Can you sense his confusion? Note the connection between "I have been serving . . ." and "you have never given . . ." To the legalist, the approval of the father is the direct result of good behavior, which explains his bewilderment at the younger son's receiving a party after such bad behavior. This perspective overestimates the good we do and fails to comprehend the very quality that sets our God apart from all false gods: grace.

Before beginning your hunt for legalists, consider these penetrating words:

This boy did all the right things. He was obedient, dutiful, law abiding, and hardworking. People respected him, admired him, praised him, and likely considered him a model son. Outwardly, the elder son was faultless. But when confronted by his father's joy at the return of his younger brother, a dark power erupts in him and boils to the surface. Suddenly, there becomes glaringly visible a resentful, proud, unkind, selfish person, one that had remained deeply hidden, even though it had been growing stronger and more powerful over the years.

Looking deeply into myself and then around me at the lives of others, I wonder what does more damage, lust or resentment? There's so much resentment among the "just" and the "righteous." So much judgment, condemnation, and prejudice among the "saints." There's so much hidden anger among the people who are so concerned about avoiding "sin."

The lostness of the resentful "saint" is so hard to reach precisely because it is so closely wedded to the desire to be good and virtuous.[7]

And he said to him, "Son, you have always been with me, and all that is mine is yours. But we had to celebrate and rejoice, for this brother of yours was dead and has begun to live, and was lost and has been found." (Luke 15:31–32)

Shakespeare wrote in one of his sonnets, "Love is not love which alters when it alteration finds." The grace of the father is truly amazing. His love is not altered by encountering this boy. He showed the older son the same gentleness he gave the younger. He even acknowledged his "faithfulness" and showed him appreciation. Yet the older brother's attitude would not allow him to receive and accept his father's grace. His desire to make himself worthy of the father's love *in his own eyes* prevented him from seeing his need for it, and so he failed to relish the love he had been given all along.

Note how the father referred to the prodigal: "this brother of yours." The legalist didn't acknowledge his kinship earlier, but the father was not about to let him forget it. He also wanted his older son to turn his focus away from himself and begin to value the same thing the father does, a relationship with his children. "This brother of yours was dead and has begun to live, and was lost and has been found." But legalists cannot see anything beyond themselves. They only pretend to value what God values by pretending to love righteousness. But if their hearts truly beat with His, they would join the party when the unrighteous repent. Let's face it; legalists rarely party.

The Roles We Play

In the three roles portrayed in Jesus's family story, I find three principles that apply to you and me, regardless of our age or gender or situation. Each of us can be found in each of the three roles—the father, the older brother, and the prodigal.

First, *we all have enough of the younger brother's rebellion in us that it should keep us from judging and criticizing anybody.* Each one of us emerged from our mother's womb a rebel. As I carefully explained in an earlier chapter, we're completely corrupted by sin from the very moment of conception. As soon as we could make responsible decisions, we took our Father's treasure and foolishly squandered it so that we have nothing to offer Him upon our return. Any righteous deeds we bring bear the stench of our own pigsty.

Fortunately, our Father wants nothing more than our return. He waits, looking on the horizon for our familiar gait. He longs to meet our repentance with a flood of kisses, a robe, a ring, a pair of shoes, and a celebration with His heavenly host. Grace awaits us. If you haven't turned to Him in simple, child-like faith, I invite you now. If you don't know the right words, make the prodigal's your own: "Father, I have sinned against heaven and in your sight; I am no longer worthy to be called your [child]" (Luke 15:21). God has already promised to receive you and give you unmerited favor, forgiveness through the sacrificial death of His Son, Jesus, and eternal life through His resurrection from the dead. Don't wait. Don't try to improve yourself first. Come to Him just as you are.

If, today, you are wearing a robe, a ring, and shoes you don't deserve, received by the Father's grace, never, ever forget your pigsty. If you are truly repentant and genuinely related to the Father again, you can't even condemn the Pharisee for his self-righteous blindness. You will see that he, too, needs the Father's compassion.

Second, *we all have so much of the older brother's pride in us that we could also be just as mean-spirited and hypocritical.* Most of us are insecure enough to elevate our own position at the expense of another. So we cluck our tongues and wag our heads at the foolishness of the grace-killing older brother, yet deep down, we conceal a pride that's no less insidious. Let me urge you to be honest enough to face the fact that the last time someone we didn't particularly like took a moral tumble, we stood a little taller in our own minds, right? Rather than grieving the fall of a fellow prodigal, we took it as an opportunity to tally another merit point on our side of the column. Don't look now, but could that be a hint of mud under our robes of righteousness?

It's also very probable that you have a Pharisee living in your home, perhaps a son or daughter, a parent, or even a spouse. You and I can do nothing to change a Pharisee; it's a problem of the heart that only the Lord can fix. However, you can do as Jesus did. Keep the truth out in plain sight for everyone to see. Acknowledge at least one claim of the legalist; you *don't* deserve the love and the favor of God. You *are* an unworthy sinner; however, you are also a son. God has provided you a ring and a pair of sandals to prove it. Don't be ashamed of your unworthiness; it proclaims the grace of God all the louder. It is a truth that has the power to set the legalist free, if only he will join the party. Don't preach. Don't rebuff. Don't justify yourself. Simply live the truth of your freedom openly and joyously, not out of spite, but in love.

Third, *we all need more of the Father's grace in us.* Though we are sons, returned to our place of privilege and intimacy with the Father, we have a responsibility to pass that grace on to our own children and friends. The father in Jesus's parable was secure enough to release his short-sighted boy without an argument. He was strong enough to wait for his return with great patience. He was faithful enough to keep praying and watching despite the lack of visible hope. He was forgiving enough to receive his son without browbeating or lecturing upon his return. He was generous enough to restore his boy to his former place of honor, despite how little he deserved. He was gracious enough to plead for the older son's humility. Grace saturated his every word and deed, yet I must point out, he never lowered his standards or set aside his love for righteousness. For the father, unlike the older brother, grace and righteousness are not mortal enemies.

As a parent, you will have both of these children living in your house, often within the same person! Both need the firm yet graceful involvement of the prodigal's father.

In his insightful book *What's So Amazing About Grace?* Philip Yancey tells the true story of a prostitute who lived on the streets. She sat before a man who worked with the indigent of Chicago admitting that she couldn't make enough money selling herself to support her drug habit, so she started renting out her daughter—only two years old—to especially depraved men interested in that sort of thing. His friend reported the abuse, of course, and rescued the child. But during his encounter, he asked if she had considered going to a church for help.

"I will never forget the look of pure, naive shock that crossed her face. 'Church!' she cried. 'Why would I ever go there? I was already feeling terrible about myself. They'd just make me feel worse.'"

What struck me about my friend's story is that women much like this prostitute fled toward Jesus, not away from him.[8]

What if she had come to your church? Or how about your home? What if she were your daughter? What kind of welcome would she have received? Does grace characterize your home, or is your approval conditional? Do your children know that you love them apart from any good or bad deeds they do? Have you allowed a Pharisee to control your home? Probing deeper, are *you* that Pharisee? I challenge you to confront those "older brother attitudes"—even if you find them in yourself—with the plain, simple, loving, graceful truth. And as you do, remind yourself of the words of Jesus again and again:

IF THE SON MAKES YOU FREE, YOU WILL BE FREE INDEED.
(JOHN 8:36)

NINE

Increasing the Priority of Your Family

*I*t's time to go home.

I don't mean in your car; I mean in your heart. When you go home in your heart, you acknowledge the priority of your family and you underscore its value. Your life declares to all who observe your habits that these people are more important to you than anything else on earth. They deserve your time and devotion. They help you to remain sensible, real, and accountable. The interaction you enjoy with your family strengthens your character so that you are better able to face a corrupt culture with integrity.

Family advocate and author Gary Bauer issued a similar call in his book *Our Journey Home*:

> Could it be that we need humbly to "go home"? For more than thirty years now we have tossed off many of the rules and restraints painfully learned by trial and error through thousands of years of civilization. Thinking we could have

it all and do it all, we went on the equivalent of a national binge. Instead of self-sacrifice, our culture has elevated self-fulfillment as the theme of the hour. Responsibility has been de-emphasized, while at the same time we have created whole new categories of rights—usually rights to unlimited self-expression or some form of self-destructive behavior. Virtue was put on the shelf and blushing (as Mark Twain wrote, humans are the only animals that can blush, or need to) became passé. Faced with an epidemic of vene-real disease, our cultural gurus, from Hollywood to the sports arenas, urge us to worship at the altar of "safe sex."

Now we've awakened with a monstrous hangover. Our schools don't work. Our children are worse off than they were thirty years ago. Over a quarter of them are born out of wedlock. Family breakup is at record levels. Taxes are high, but the government wants even more revenue. The federal budget deficit is out of sight, and many state budg-ets are as bad or worse. The streets are not safe. In some of our gunfire-wracked cities, even the bassinets aren't safe. We have less time with our families. Even with all the extra hours we spend in the workplace, we're falling behind competitively.

If ever there were a time to go home, this is it.

Some pessimists argue that going home is impossible after this many years on the wrong side of town. We've been away too long, they say. The old house is boarded up, and the folks have moved away and left no forwarding address.[1]

I can't say I entirely agree with the pessimism in Bauer's piece. I have two objections. First, I don't think the human heart has gotten any worse. It has been completely corrupt since the first humans committed the first sin. Second, I do think we have the ability to make our world a better place to live. I am a realist, so I know that sin will always have the potential to destroy people's lives, families, and communities. But I am also an optimist. I believe that as people submit to the Lord completely, they place greater priority on their families. If enough do that, it would radically transform our world. That's not just wishful thinking; that's the message of Scripture. Candidly, if I didn't believe that things can be better, I couldn't be in ministry, and I certainly couldn't preach the Word of God with any sense of confidence and hope.

Throughout history, great societies have come and gone. And according to the research of some impressive minds in the field of sociology, the strength of individual families almost always played a decisive role in the success of a culture. While I believe the institution of the family can be strengthened, Gary Bauer is right—the present trend doesn't look good. The respective roles of husband and wife have become so blurred, many men and women don't know what they should be doing to fulfill them. Many parents can't define their roles in the lives of their children beyond the provision of shelter, clothing, and three meals a day. Many children have no idea who they are, why they are important, or how they could contribute to their world. Not surprisingly, the importance of community has all but vanished. The concept of helping a neighbor has become a quaint notion from a bygone era. You have to *know* your neighbor before you can help him or her. How can we do that with an eight-foot privacy fence separating us?

Now, let's be honest. People *say* they value family above career and personal fulfillment, but how connected are they to the other people living under their roof? Let me make this more personal. If it weren't for cell phones and text messaging, how much contact would you have with your children? When was the last time you spent a solid thirty minutes deliberately nurturing someone bearing your genes?

I know we still have the potential to give priority to our families. While the human heart has been corrupted by sin, it still longs for the stability, nurturing, and guidance that families provide. As we race toward the future, we cannot help but feel the tension growing in our ties to the past. At the risk of sounding dated, we long for the values of our forefathers—family values, if you will. Clearly defined standards of right and wrong. Closeness at home, reverence at church, safety at school and in the neighborhood, fair play at work, and common sense in the courtroom. Perhaps that's why the gentle-sounding country song "Grandpa" became such a hit.

> Grandpa, tell me 'bout the good old days.
> Sometimes it feels like the world's gone crazy.
> Grandpa, tell me, take me back to yesterday,
> When the line between right and wrong didn't
>   seem so hazy.
> Did lovers really fall in love to stay,

Stand beside each other come what may?
Was a promise really something people kept,
Not just something they would say?
Did families really bow their heads to pray?
Did daddies really never go away?
Oh, Grandpa,
Tell me 'bout the good old days.[2]

Besides the basic desire we have for strong families and solid communities, the primary reason for my optimism is Scripture. One of the rewards of remaining committed to the Word of God is that you have at your fingertips absolute, God-breathed truth. It's always timely, completely reliable, clearly relevant, and thoroughly applicable. Though nearly three millennia have passed since they were composed, my optimism for our future comes from Psalms 127 and 128.

An Ancient Family Hymn

Within the hymnbook of the Psalms, we find fifteen short songs, Psalms 120–134, comprising a section called by many the "Little Psalter." Ancient Hebrew editors added a superscript to these psalms that reads, "A Song of the Ascents." Most English versions of the Bible place this in italics just beneath the psalm number, rendering it either "A Song of Ascents" or "A Song of Degrees." But the Hebrew includes a definite article, which I believe to be significant.

No one knows for sure why they are called ascent psalms, though theories abound. The most credible theory makes the best sense of the definite article in the superscript. When a Jewish man approached Solomon's temple, he supposedly ascended fifteen stairs leading to the vestibule. Tradition holds that on each of the three annual festivals, a faithful Jew paused on each step to recite or sing the corresponding psalm. Most of them, though short, reflect upon virtually every important facet of life for the Jewish community. Not surprisingly, the middle two, Psalms 127 and 128, contemplate the Lord's relationship with the family and how important a healthy, godly family is to the prosperity of the nation.

Putting them together reminds me of a historical monument near Houston, Texas. The stately San Jacinto Monument features a giant mural that stitches together several depictions of key events in chronological order, tracing the history of Texas. These two psalms form a literary mural, tracing the most important events in the life of the family. As we walk around this monument, we'll see a married couple establish their home, give birth to children, nurture and rear them in close association with the Lord, and finally release them to have children of their own. The inspired mural depicts a flourishing family as God intended, a family whose members place the highest priority on Him and on each other. If we observe closely, we'll discover three important principles and two crucial reminders along the way.

THREE FOUNDATIONAL PRINCIPLES

Psalm 127 opens with a foundational principle upon which everything else is built.

> Unless the LORD builds the house,
> They labor in vain who build it;
> Unless the LORD guards the city,
> The watchman keeps awake in vain.
> It is vain for you to rise up early,
> To retire late,
> To eat the bread of painful labors;
> For He gives to His beloved even in his sleep.
> (Psalm 127:1–2)

The Hebrew language has at least two ways to emphasize a point. The first is to repeat a term or a phrase. The second is to change the usual order of the words in the sentence structure by moving the emphasized words to the beginning of the sentence. And if they wanted to make the point especially strong, they employed both methods. In this case, the literal Hebrew for the first two lines would read,

> If the Lord builds not the house, *in vain* the builders labored.
>   If the Lord guards not the city, *in vain* has watched the guard.

To the ancient Hebrew, the term *house* meant more than a physical structure. In the Old Testament, a house represented the family and, more significantly, the family's legacy—the prosperity and the social standing of future generations. Builders can construct a palatial house, but if the Lord isn't crafting the family

185

inside, every square foot of that magnificent structure is wasted space.

The first principle: *it is futile to build a home or a family using human effort alone.* Note the repeated phrase "unless the Lord." To give your family higher priority, you must keep the Lord in first place. Put the Lord at the center of your relationships and let your devotion to Him permeate every segment of your home life.

The great temptation is to fill the bookshelves with how-to manuals, to learn and apply tips, tricks, and techniques. While I'm a big believer in the science of psychology and the value of family counseling, any truth these professionals discover belongs to God. Therefore, we can utilize that knowledge to our benefit. However, no human author and no tried-and-true techniques can substitute for an authentic relationship with the living God. Without Him, we too easily try to build a house using human strength for selfish reasons or for the purpose of impressing others.

Over the years, Cynthia and I have built a few houses. One of our builders (whom we later released) seemed determined to build our house for the sake of its visitors instead of its residents. After describing a particular feature, he said, "Don't you want this in the entrance?"

"No, we don't want that," I replied.

He insisted. "Oh, but all the other houses in the neighborhood have this!"

To which I responded, "Makes me want it even less."

"Are you certain? Now, when you come in, you could have so-and-so. That would make a great impression."

"I'm not interested in making a great impression. I'm interested in building the house *we* want."

"But," he said, "think of all the people who will be coming."

"Really, we're the ones who will be living here. It's not about what anyone else thinks." Then I said, "By the way, do most of your clients care that much about what other people think?"

He said, "Actually, about ninety percent of the people who want me to build their houses, build them to impress other people—their neighbors, their guests."

How silly is that? Why would I want to live in a house other people like? And here's the real kicker: many of those same people are paying far more than they can afford, so they end up enslaved to the bank and a second job. They moonlight their children's lives away, thinking, *Look at me. I'm a big-time provider. They have nice things because I work long, hard hours.*

They have built an impressive structure, but their real house is crumbling.

Take note of the second verse: "It is vain for you to rise up early, to retire late, to eat the bread of painful labors; for He gives to His beloved even in his sleep."

The temptation is to think that if we work hard enough, earn enough academic degrees, or put in long enough hours, and make enough money, we can eventually get far enough ahead to cut back later. But thinking anything in those categories will ever be "enough" is the self-delusion of the work-obsessed person who sacrifices a thousand sunny days for that one potential rainy day. His or her temptation is to add hours to their day and days to their weeks, to rise early and go to bed late, to choke down fast food on the way from one task to another, to get the top position, to feel satisfied only with the spoils of hard labor.

If that describes you, I have this one-word piece of advice: STOP! Don't even thank God for that stuff. You didn't receive it from Him; you pursued it at the expense of your family. That's the life of one who is building his or her house by human strength without looking to the Lord to build it. And the Lord of our lives calls that kind of building futile. Remember? "It is vain . . ."

The psalmist declares that when the Lord takes over the construction process, the owners sleep like babies. They prosper even as they enjoy a good night's sleep, while the work-obsessed continue the grind. And let's face it, the work-obsessed love their hard labor; they're only satisfied with those things that remind them of their sweat and toil. Free gifts from the hand of God feel too much like cheating.

Let me probe a little deeper by asking you several questions. If you value the things you have earned more than the things you received by grace from the hand of God, how might that affect your priorities? Family? Finances? The Lord's place in your home? This leads to the second principle.

The Lord must have first priority over everything, including the house and the family. This typically impacts the budget in two important ways. First, it demands that we look to the Lord for our income. He may use a career or wise investments to supply our material needs, but we must never confuse the gift with the Giver. This priority comes into play when we consider a career move—whether it will take us to where no good church can be found or involves a significant demand on our time and energy.

Though the salary doubles, the cost may be the Lord's primacy in our house.

Second, it challenges us to plan our giving. Let me clarify that the Lord does not need our money. He already owns the entire universe, including everything we have in our possession. Anything we hold must be considered a loan. So let's not allow ourselves to think we're doing Him any favors. The challenge to give forces us to clarify our priorities. When we respond to God's invitation to join Him in accomplishing what only He can do, when we invest our money in the kingdom rather than satisfy a want, we declare that He has precedence over our own desires.

While Psalm 127:1–2 describes the establishment of a bride and a groom establishing their new home, verses 3 to 5 continue the family mural with the addition of little ones. And they point to a third principle: *As children come, each is to be treasured as God's gift and given priority over our vocation or personal fulfillment.*

> Behold, children are a gift of the LORD,
> The fruit of the womb is a reward.
> Like arrows in the hand of a warrior,
> So are the children of one's youth.
> How blessed is the man whose quiver is full of them;
> They will not be ashamed
> When they speak with their enemies in the gate.
> (Psalm 127:3–5)

Take note of the link between verses 2 and 3:

For He gives to His beloved . . .
. . . children are a gift of the LORD.

As I review the images the Lord uses to describe children, I don't read "tax deduction," "interruption," "accident," "mouth to feed," "hassle," "challenge," or "fetal tissue." I see terms that describe each child as God's special gift, an asset that will enrich a house and bring it honor. The picture of children as arrows might seem strange to our Western, twenty-first-century perspective, but people in the ancient world could not look to civil government to feed them and protect them. They depended upon their family, their "house." A strong family provided safety, provision, and companionship, as well as a sense of identity and belonging. On the other hand, to be without a family was to be completely and literally helpless.

To put this in more contemporary terms, think of a modern soldier in battle carrying a high-powered rifle with a fully loaded magazine, a .45 semi automatic handgun on his hip, and a satchel full of ammunition. That's the picture of a man who means business. He's powerful. He's intimidating. He doesn't have to worry about being mugged! In a similar way, anyone who might want to take advantage of a family would think twice about a couple who had been blessed with a houseful of strapping, strong-hearted sons and intelligent, industrious daughters.

To continue the metaphor, arrows are sharp, delicate, dangerous objects. At a camp for teenagers, I once took an archery lesson that could have been disastrous. After my first four tries, the instructor cleared the area and stood behind me with the other cringing onlookers as I tried to guide an arrow home. With a target about the size of a king-sized mattress and standing fewer than fifty feet away, I finally managed to hit the edge.

Arrows in the hands of a skilled archer can feed and defend the household, but few things are more deadly than a misdirected arrow. The same can be said of confused, undisciplined, and misdirected children. Learning to guide a child requires concentration, diligence, a willingness to look foolish, plenty of practice, and patience—lots of patience.

I have been blessed with four very sharp arrows. I originally thought our quiver was built for two. One boy and one girl—Alpha and Omega, the beginning and the end. Then we moved to New England (where it snows a lot) and along came our third. Soon after we returned to our home state of Texas, we had our fourth. Obviously the Lord intended for us to have more gifts that we anticipated, but, in all honesty, I cannot imagine life without our four God-given children! How much poorer the world would have been without each one. The Lord placed those four arrows in the trembling hands of a father-warrior to direct them carefully and well. To say that I have been blessed would qualify as the understatement of the year.

Take note of the concluding thoughts in the psalm:

How blessed is the man whose quiver is full of them;
They will not be ashamed
When they speak with their enemies in the gate.
(Psalm 127:5)

The last two sentences describe how the parents and the children enjoy a mutual benefit from their relationship. The parents are blessed by having a full quiver of arrows, but "they"—that is, the children—will not be ashamed when they must defend the family in public.

The city gate customarily served as the community courthouse. There, city leaders gathered to discuss civil order, hear and decide disputes, witness and seal contracts. This was a place to speak with one's enemies in public in order to conduct business and settle disagreements. If our children have been guided well, they will stand on their own with the security and the confidence of a strong house. They will have received the heritage of a respected family name. A strong "house," built by the Lord and nurtured by parents having clear priorities, gives children the best foundation to enjoy security and success in life.

Two Crucial Reminders

Many believe that the Hebrew editors specifically chose and arranged these fifteen individual songs to form a progression, and the close association of Psalms 127 and 128 helps to support the idea. Psalm 128:1 picks up the same words that begin Psalm 127:5: "How blessed is the one . . ." The mural continues with scenes of a growing, thriving family. The Lord establishes and builds the house, filling it with children. In this scene, He's the center of life.

How blessed is everyone who fears the LORD,
Who walks in His ways.

When you shall eat of the fruit of your hands,
You will be happy and it will be well with you.
Your wife shall be like a fruitful vine
Within your house,
Your children like olive plants
Around your table.
Behold, for thus shall the man be blessed
Who fears the LORD.
(Psalm 128:1–4)

What a picture of a flourishing family! "Fear," in this case, refers to the healthy reverence of the Lord that results in obedience. This is not the fear we have for tornadoes or heart attacks. God isn't standing over us wielding a board with a nail in it, waiting for us to fail. Fear of reprisal doesn't motivate anyone's obedience. The fear that causes a home to flourish looks more like awe.

My father and mother used to say, "Ours is a God-fearing home." By that, they meant to remind us that everything we say and do reflects upon our relationship with the Lord. We recognize Him as the sovereign king of our house. I learned early to respect His name and to guard against using it flippantly or profanely. I learned to respect the place of worship and to commit the songs of worship to memory. I learned to approach His Word with a spirit of wonder that still overtakes me today. I learned from my mom and dad to thank Him for every good thing, however great or small, and also to accept the hard times without complaining.

When a relationship with the Lord is the first priority of the home—above everything else, including career or even ministry—He brings prosperity and well-being to everyone in it. Note the features of a God-worshiping home as the passage addresses the man.

He will find satisfaction in his work rather than frustration, and when he works he will be happy and secure, instead of frazzled and burned out. Furthermore, his wife and children will thrive. The images of a fruitful vine and clustered olive branches symbolized peace and security in ancient Israel. Vineyards and olive groves take a long time to cultivate, requiring years of tending before producing the first useful fruit. Only a land that enjoys plenty of rain, a good climate, and freedom from warfare or internal conflict can produce grapes and olives. When a husband looks to the Lord to protect and nurture his home, he enjoys a wife described as a lush, fruitful vine and children around his table like clusters of olive-laden branches. This is a lovely picture of peace and prosperity.

I think this word picture from the agricultural world runs deeper than the simplistic, self-serving promise "Worship Me, and I'll give you lots of money." First, I find nothing monetary about the blessings, though money is not excluded. The man will find satisfaction in his work as he looks to the Lord—not to the job—for provision and protection. The woman enjoys the careful, gentle, conscientious tending and affirmation of her husband, which allow her to flourish. The children gather around the family table like olive branches, an image that symbolized peace, the faithful remnant of Israel.

I have to admit, I know almost nothing about horticulture. I have to pay a landscaper to keep my lawn and planting beds from looking like a desert. In fact, he's said to me more than once, "I suggest you stay away from the plants." He knows me well. However, I do know this much: healthy plants don't just happen. They require knowledge and nurturing to stay green and growing.

Years ago, I knew a fine landscaper by the name of Manny. Curious about his talent, I asked, "How do you do it? Everything I touch turns brown."

He kindly responded, "I study plants, I learn what they like best, I experiment and watch their response, and . . . well, I talk to them."

"You're kidding me."

"No," he said. Then, pointing to an azalea loaded with blossoms, he said, "I actually sing to this one."

Okay, I have to admit, I had heard of this before but I didn't give it much credence, and the science behind the theory proved to be pretty flimsy. But it did occur to me that the kind of person who would take time to talk to a plant would be a particularly sensitive horticulturist by nature. The serenading probably does nothing, but a singing landscaper can work miracles with plants. That much I've seen in person, which points to the first of two important reminders: *A happy home doesn't just happen; it's the result of giving the Lord top priority and investing time and attention in the family.*

Barbara Bush delivered the 1990 commencement address at the notoriously feminist Wellesley College. Many of the students protested the school's choice of speaker. They didn't deem her worthy of the honor since she had chosen motherhood and homemaking as her vocation instead of pursuing a career outside the home. Despite the objections, Mrs. Bush decided to capitalize on what she considered a teachable moment.

Cherish your human connections: your relationships with family and friends. For several years, you've had impressed upon you the importance to your career of dedication and hard work, and, of course, that's true. But as important as your obligations as a doctor, lawyer or business leader will be, you are a human being first and those human connections—with spouses, with children, with friends—are the most important investments you will ever make.

At the end of your life, you will never regret not having passed one more test, not winning one more verdict or not closing one more deal. You will regret time not spent with a husband, a child, a friend or a parent. . . .

Whatever the era, whatever the times, one thing will never change: Fathers and mothers, if you have children— they must come first.

You must read to your children, hug your children, and you must love your children. Your success as a family . . . our success as a society depends not on what happens in the White House, but on what happens inside your house.[3]

Psalm 128 builds to a crescendo with a blessing in verses 5 to 6:

The LORD bless you from Zion,

And may you see the prosperity of Jerusalem all the days
of your life.

Indeed, may you see your children's children.

Peace be upon Israel!

(Psalm 128:5–6)

I often pray that I'll never become hard to live with. I hope
that our children will want to be around me regardless of my
age . . . that the grandkids will want to move in with us!

This final scene on the family mural reflects a house in later
life. The olive branches have borne fruit. The children have
married and have begun to prosper on their own. They're
productive, healthy, secure, strong, and happy. The old couple
have done the very best possible service to their community and
their country. They have established a strong, God-worshiping
house, nurtured their young men and women, and released them
to live on their own to establish their own strong, God-worshiping
homes. These parents deserve the benediction: "The Lord bless
you, may you reap the reward of a prosperous Israel, and may you
see your children prosper as you have." *Shalom al-Israel!*

Shalom, by the way, includes much more than the idea of
peace. It also carries the ideas of prosperity, completeness, sound-
ness, safety, health, security, and friendship. To bid someone *shalom*
is to wish upon him or her the greatest possible state of well-being
and joy. When we experience the wonders of heaven, we will have
finally found the true meaning of *shalom.* The Lord's blessing to a
strong, God-worshiping family becomes *shalom to Israel!*

The second reminder: *when we give priority to the family, the community prospers.* Can you imagine the transforming effect on your neighborhood if everyone gave greater priority to their families? We would build gates into our fences. We would build walkways to one another's homes. We would rally to protect our neighbors because someone tried to hurt one of our own. We would be mutually accountable . . . love would flow. Then each of those families would produce a number of other houses built by the Lord, and then those would reproduce. Before too many generations, a whole nation could be transformed! I am convinced that this was the Lord's plan for Canaan, starting with the Great Exodus from Egypt and His words to that first generation of Israelites about to receive the Promised Land. He said, "Hear, O Israel. The LORD is our God, the LORD is one! You shall love the LORD your God with all your heart and with all your soul and with all your might" (Deuteronomy 6:4–5).

HOW TO INCREASE THE PRIORITY OF YOUR FAMILY

The issue of any good Scripture lesson always comes down to the same little word: *how?* Like most matters of faith, the answers are simple to understand and difficult to carry out. To help you remember them I've boiled them down to four two-word challenges.

First, *think family.* Before you move, before you accept the promotion, before you commit yourself to the big project or the extra job or the tight deadline, think family. Ask yourself, *Which will do my spouse and children greater good: the extra money or my personal involvement in their lives?* Sometimes, admittedly, the better option is to earn the extra money. Provision is an important part of your role as a parent. However, how often do you take the extra assignment or the greater responsibility at work without stopping to ask the hard question? How often does the priority of your family drop down the list whenever a new career-building opportunity presents itself?

Before you make that big purchase, before you commit to those payments, how many hours will it require away from the family to earn back the money? Place those hours of investment in your family on the scale opposite the benefit of the purchase. To which side does the balance tip? Which takes priority?

Second, *say no. No* quite possibly can be the most powerful and liberating word you can add to your vocabulary. Unfortunately, two difficult issues make this a rare word on the lips of many parents: people pleasing and the fear of being rude.

No one likes to disappoint others, especially friends and people we respect. We're so afraid that by saying no, we'll damage the relationship or disappoint the other so much that we'll never recover the trust. So, if this helps, try putting it this way, either aloud or to yourself: *I'm not saying no to you. I'm saying yes to my child. I need to spend that time with him or her.*

Unfortunately, overcommitment has become so accepted, so expected in our culture that many consider it rude to refuse a request without having a compelling excuse. People have no idea what to do with a simple, polite, pleasantly delivered *no.* Try it sometime. The next time you receive a telemarketing call, just decide that your only response will be a friendly, good-natured, "No, thank you." No explanations. No excuses. No anger. No uneasiness. No justifying, arguing, or rationalizing. Just, "No, thank you." And repeat it as often as necessary. See what happens. (They won't make it easy, so this is great practice.)

Then, when you've built up the nerve, try it with someone face-to-face when you need to turn down an obligation. "No, I'm sorry but I can't at this time. Maybe another time." Again, no explanations. No excuses. No justifying, arguing, or rationalizing. Be kind. Be pleasant. But, above all, be resolved. It won't be easy, but your practice with telemarketers will have served you well.

Third, *take time*. The purpose of saying no to competing priorities is to say yes to your family. Turn off the television. Read together. Play together. Take a walk, ask some questions, discuss issues, discover one another's hopes, fears, favorite colors, or fondest memories. Get out of the house and do something unusual, or if you're never at home together, maybe you should stay home.

Recently a longtime friend of mine lay in a hospital bed. Death had taken his wife sometime earlier and he had a close brush with it himself. At one point he caught my eyes with his and said, "Chuck, stay close to Cynthia. Take time for her." I knew to take that advice seriously from a widower with a scar down the middle of his chest. Time had a very different meaning for him. The urgency in his voice and the passion in his words shook me to my senses. Isn't it easy to lose our way in the busyness of life?

The time won't offer itself freely. You have to be deliberate and tough on yourself. Don't fool yourself into thinking it'll be better once your current project is complete, or when they hire that other person they've been promising, or once the economy turns around, or after the . . . It won't happen. You will have to claim the time—and it will require you to sacrifice something significant in exchange. It always does. So please do take time.

Fourth, *be patient.* Don't expect that months or years of a longstanding habit will be undone in a week or that intimacy will instantly dispel awkwardness once you decide to be present with those in your family. No one builds a house in a single day. Begin slowly; give your family time to readjust. You might start by attending their games, plays, or band performances. Work up to taking a child to dinner, just the two of you or with you and your spouse. Then perhaps enjoy all-day outings or play dates where you do something fun together. These things have a way of turning into traditions that your family will cherish for years to come. But don't expect it all to jell overnight. Take the long-range view; build steadily and deliberately. And be patient.

Is it time for you to go home? If you're not sure, then maybe it's time to ask your spouse and children some vulnerable questions. "Do you feel more important than my career? If spending more time together meant we had to move to a smaller home or trade down to a less expensive car, would you be willing? Do you feel that I know you? In your opinion, how central is the Lord in our household?"

Perhaps the time to ask those questions is now, before you're

staring at a hospital ceiling. And should that be your experience, your bed will be encircled by people begging you to pull
through because you
    thought family,
       said no,
          took time,
             and remained patient.

             Now, please . . . go home.

TEN

Restoring Relationships After You've Blown It

Tonight you get to enjoy a rare treat. You have plans to join some friends for dinner. You meet at a favorite, comfortable restaurant and take pleasure in its warm, understated atmosphere and excellent food, prepared and served to be enjoyed throughout the entire evening. You linger over coffee and conversation long after the dishes have been cleared, and the wait staff doesn't seem to mind. Meanwhile, the restaurant slowly empties. Finally, you rise, stretch, bid your dinner companions farewell, and step out into the perfectly calm night air. You instinctively look up to see a billion stars scattered across the black canopy overhead, and as you draw in a long, deep breath, you think, *What a perfect evening.* And it was. Good food, good friends, good conversation . . . good life.

As you slip behind the wheel, you take the pleasant route home . . . slowly . . . with the windows down. Soon after rounding the last curve before your street, a strange odor hits the back of your throat. A harsh, ominous glow rises from behind the trees in your neighborhood—a bright white light punctuated by regular flashes of red, blue, and yellow.

While you were gone, your kitchen conspired against you. A freakish, almost impossible combination of a common household lubricant, paper towels, and a faulty outlet. A spark, a flicker, a fire. Unfortunately, your neighbors had turned in early. Others were out of town. And before anyone knew anything, flames were leaping from an upstairs window. By the time an elderly man walking his dog turned the corner, the inferno had engulfed your home. His call to the fire department prevented other homes from burning, but yours is a complete loss. All you have left, other than your car and the clothes on your back, is a cement slab covered with black rubble; a stark, naked chimney reaching up into the smoky air; and the charred remains of everything you owned, including the cell phone you left at home so you wouldn't be disturbed.

As the rescue workers pack up their gear, a kind face covered in soot says, "I'm sorry we couldn't do more. I'm afraid you've lost everything."

Actually, that isn't true. At least I hope not for you. The fire failed to consume two important and permanent possessions: your memories and your relationships.

If this tragedy had been yours, you would have indeed lost everything that once had a price tag—your residence, your furniture, your clothes, your other car, and your entertainment toys. But what about the memories? The laughter you shared with loved ones, the family and friends you entertained, the countless memories with your children: diapers, formula, first steps and first words, birthdays, scraped knees, soccer games, dance recitals, first love, first heartbreak, celebrations, sorrows, senior prom, the day it first dawned on you that your child will be leaving, the countdown to graduation . . .

Memories never perish, and they have the power to transform a house into a home. Fire may consume the wood, hay, and stubble of life, but all the memories remain, untouched and undisturbed. That is, if you were careful to make them. Memories rarely make themselves. The quantity and quality of your memories are the measure of a life well lived, and they are built upon moments in time shared with those you love—time spent *with* them, not tasks done *for* them.

Did you catch that? Look back on your life. Take a few moments to do it now. I'll wait . . .

What did you recall? Moments or tasks? Accomplishments or people? Chances are good you reflected on some of the more significant experiences you shared with the people you have loved the longest and cherished the most. Maybe you were a little dismayed to discover that much of your life has blank spaces where memories should have gone, times when you were busy clicking off tasks. People in that situation try to convince themselves that what they did, they did for family, but it rings hollow in the absence of meaningful memories.

Tragedy has an amazing way of clarifying one's priorities.

Let's go back to the house fire. As you stare at the water-soaked remains of everything tangible that meant anything to you, a sweet peace falls on the dismal scene as you think, *Thank you, Lord, that no one was home.* The memories are important because the people with whom you made them are important. Relationships not only survive disasters such as this, but they tend to deepen. That is, if you have kept them in good repair. But then, let's be honest here . . . maybe you haven't.

What to Do After You've Blown It

Whenever I speak on the topic of family, I invariably have people—of all ages and stages of life—say something like this: "Chuck, all of this stuff you're teaching is great, but I'm hearing it a bit late. I've already made many of the mistakes you're warning against. What do I do now that I've blown it?"

That's actually a very astute question. I hear in it the earnest humility of the prodigal son, the sorrow of a man or woman who allowed the priority of family to slide from time to time— or perhaps more often than that. It's a question I can appreciate on a very personal level. What do you do when you run your fingers along the edge of your memory and you feel a snag at one particular family member—the one who suffered the most by your chronic absence, your emotional unavailability, or worse, your cruel treatment? You may have in mind a singular incident that created a breach or, like most everyone, a long-term, consistent failure to do or be as you should. Regardless, the relationship is distant or strained, mainly because of you. What now?

The desire to recover a relationship from the ashes of that emotional house fire can be expressed in one word: reconciliation. The word *reconcile* deserves some serious thought. It has a

number of nuances and uses in the English language, and from a
certain point of view, all of them come into play when applied to
relationships. Here is the entry in *Merriam-Webster's Collegiate
Dictionary*:

rec•on•cile \ re-ken-sil\ vb -ciled; -cil•ing [ME, fr. MF or L; MF
reconcilier, fr. L *reconciliare*, fr. *re-* + *conciliare* to conciliate] *vt*
(14c) **1a**: to restore to friendship or harmony <*reconciled* the
factions> **b**: SETTLE, RESOLVE <-differences> **2**: to make consistent or congruous <-an ideal with reality> **3**: to cause to submit
to or accept something unpleasant <was *reconciled* to hardship>
4a: to check (a financial account) against another for accuracy **b**:
to account for ~*vi*: to become reconciled *syn* see ADAPT—
rec•on•cil•abil•i•ty \ re-ken-si-le-bi-le-te \ *n*—rec•on•cil•able \
re-ken-si-le-bel, re-ken-/ *adj*—

Glance at each usage and apply it to the process of repairing
the breach in a significant relationship from your past. Pause
long enough to ponder some examples.

REALITY REVISITED

Now, I realize that a relationship is a bridge having two ends, not
just one, and that you can tend only yours. Only the Lord can
prompt the other person to do his or her part. So our responsibility is to begin building the bridge on our side and avoid the
temptation to toss messages over to the other, spelling out what
he or she ought to be doing. Of course, this means that you
might work yourself to the bone and still have no relationship to
show for it. But I can promise you that your efforts will not have

been in vain. God always honors faith. He never fails to meet an act of grace with more grace, one way or another.

Because any act of reconciliation is by no means a smooth, risk-free act, we have to acknowledge some unpleasant realities. These may be obvious; nevertheless, I find three reminders helpful whenever I dare to begin the reconciliation process.

First, *every person on earth is imperfect.* Isaiah 53:6 tells us, "All of us like sheep have gone astray, each of us has turned to his own way." Romans 3:23 declares, "All have sinned and fall short of the glory of God," which is a reference to Psalm 14:3: "They have all turned aside, together they have become corrupt; there is no one who does good, not even one." That includes our neighbors, our friends, our families, and certainly ourselves. Truth be told, we are selfish, proud, stubborn creatures who work to figure out life as best we can and, in the process, establish destructive habits that work well for us. And because they work, we feel sure they must be right despite the pain we cause others along the way.

Furthermore, our unwillingness to accept these imperfections keeps us stewing in our resentment, which shuts down any desire for reconciliation. When we ignore the simple fact that misunderstandings, hurt feelings, and selfishness are the norm and that unbreakable relationships don't exist, we lose our capacity for compassion. I find Brennan Manning's confession very helpful:

> The betrayals and infidelities in my life are too numerous to count. I still cling to the illusion that I must be morally impeccable, other people must be sinless, and the one I

love must be without human weakness. But whenever I allow anything but tenderness and compassion to dictate my response to life—be it self-righteous anger, moralizing, defensiveness, the pressing need to change others, carping criticism, frustration at others' blindness, a sense of spiritual superiority, a gnawing hunger of vindication—I am alienated from my true self. My identity as Abba's child becomes ambiguous, tentative, and confused.[1]

The quickest way to become a Pharisee is to deny that sin and selfishness continue to be a regular part of our daily interaction with others.

A second helpful reminder: *no person can change the past.* Don't you wish life had an "undo" button like your computer? Wouldn't you love to have a second chance with your first child? Think of how much better a parent you would have been with the knowledge you have now. But you can't un-say what you shouldn't have said. You can't re-say better what you said poorly. You can't turn back the calendar to undo past mistakes. The damage is done. The pain is palpable. The spirit remains wounded. No amount of wishing or regret will delete a sinful or unwise deed.

Again, obvious. Yet how quickly we forget that truth when remembering a past sin gives us such painful pleasure. Regret, while painful, serves an important purpose. It allows us to keep a safe distance from what we are sure will be the other person's unbridled wrath. Nevertheless, we must risk vulnerability. Wishing the past hadn't happened won't give the relationship a future.

Third, *each person is personally responsible for his or her own stuff.* We may have made a terrible mess of a relationship, and we are responsible for our part. Or the other person may have behaved intolerably and will not accept responsibility. The difficult fact we must accept is that, despite who did what or started something else, we can't fix him. We aren't responsible for her development. We can only deal with our own stuff. As we look at the restoration process, I urge you to turn your focus inward. You may have an ex-partner who left you with a shattered life and children to rear on your own. You may have a sibling who won't talk to you, much less give you a chance to rebuild. Your children may not want to have anything to do with you. Whatever your situation, however much or little you contributed to the breach, you must start with yourself. Begin by owning what's yours as though the other person were entirely innocent.

Reconciliation can be a remarkable opportunity to grow, and, as with any act of faith, it gives the Lord opportunity to reveal Himself in unusual ways. I have reconciled with a number of people whom I offended. Some of them were folks I didn't know I had offended until later. Others I had offended and, frankly, I didn't care. Finally, when God began to work on me, I didn't find them knocking on my door hoping to rebuild. I had to own all my stuff, swallow every stinking ounce of my pride, risk the confession, and ask for forgiveness.

This is especially important with our children, even before they are old enough to completely understand what we're doing. John White addressed this in his book *Parents in Pain:*

We parents are imperfect. We are imperfect not only in failing to do those things we can (which is blame-worthy) but in lacking some parental capacities entirely. We can only give what we have. We cannot give what we do not have. So our children are bound to experience deprivation because they are born to imperfect parents in a fallen world.

Never pretend to your children that you are better than you are. Let them know that you are a fellow struggler, one who may have known glorious victories but equally ignominious defeats. . . .

I do not say you are to bare your soul to your children, or to reveal to them the horrors of every pit into which you have descended. But where your conduct in the home has been blameworthy, be open about it. They must not see in you a paragon of virtue but a redeemed sinner, one who goes on learning and who refuses to be discouraged by falls. Give them someone to follow, not someone to worship.[2]

This is the cornerstone of authenticity. Without it, children have in you an impossible standard. Furthermore, they instinctively know that no one is perfect, so failing to acknowledge our failings openly, we teach them to ignore personal wrongs by covering them over.

RESPONSES TO AVOID

This leads me to share two responses that feel very natural and appropriate but will likely shut down the reconciliation process. In my experience, I have discovered that neither is helpful.

The first is saying or thinking, *It's all my fault.* Accepting complete responsibility for one's own failings will go a long way to ease tensions and give the other person space to reflect on his or her own contribution to the mess. And the process should indeed start with you, regardless of who's at fault for what. However, I have very rarely seen a situation where a broken relationship was the sole fault of one person. Furthermore, if you accept responsibility for the poor behavior of both parties, you leave the other person little opportunity to learn and grow.

As a parent, remember that children are born imperfect, which means that they will routinely fail to handle things well. And that makes parenting a demanding and complex job. Each time a child fails, the parent can always say, *I should have taught him better. I didn't warn her enough.* Please, from one parent to another, *give yourself a break.* Your child is an individual with a will, a brain, a depraved nature, and the capacity to learn from mistakes. You can lead, you can instruct, and you can reprove, but you can't change a heart or transform a mind. Only the Holy Spirit can do that. Be willing to accept responsibility for your failures and lapses when and where appropriate, but remind yourself, it's not all your fault!

A second response that will put a halt to restoring a relationship is the simplistic use of Bible verses, both with yourself and with others. Parents are particularly susceptible to this with regard to verses like the proverb we studied earlier:

"Train up a child in the way he should go, Even when he is old he will not depart from it" (Proverbs 22:6).

A simplistic approach would be to read into that verse a

promise, then expect an airtight, never-fail, lifetime guarantee that each child will turn out perfectly. This sets the standards for successful childrearing unrealistically, impossibly high, and, furthermore, it suggests that the process of training a child is no more difficult than following a recipe. Worst of all, it sets up the parent for terrible disappointment and guilt when the child eventually blows it. Our Bible does contain promises, but we have to be careful to read them only where God makes them. Proverbs are excellent principles for living, but we live in a complex, sinful world where things often don't go according to a precise plan. Furthermore, a Bible verse doesn't substitute for wisdom. Scripture is to be taken in, meditated upon, applied, and made available to the Holy Spirit as He transforms you. As you grow in wisdom, you will develop greater ability to lead your child.

FIVE STEPS TO RECONCILIATION
AFTER YOU'VE BLOWN IT

The section title sounds simple, doesn't it? Five steps and that's it? We've built the bridge? We've closed that huge gap between us? Let me caution you not to mistake simple with easy. The strategies I find in Isaiah 58 are not complicated, but they are far from easy to carry out. As I explain them, please commit yourself to the following:

First, *avoid the temptation to apply them simplistically.* There's no easy-to-follow, quick recipe for restoring a relationship. These are principles that, when applied, will give your relationship the best chance of renewal. However, you can't predict how someone else will react. He or she may not respond right away, or even after you have tried several times. All you can do is your best. So guard against a simplistic mindset.

Second, *read these words with someone particular in mind and a plan to reconcile with him or her.* As you determine to bridge the gap between the two of you, begin with the helpful steps we uncover.

HOW THE PEOPLE OF JUDAH BLEW IT

The prophet Isaiah lived in the southern region of the kingdom of Judah. At this point in Hebrew history, the people had reduced the worship of God to rote formula. They went through empty repeated motions, they gave their offerings much as we would pay our taxes, and they prided themselves on their faithfulness. However, their hearts were as cold and hard as stone. In this environment of phony, self-centered religiosity, the Lord called Isaiah to do what prophets do best: comfort the afflicted and afflict the comfortable.

In Isaiah 58:1–4, God instructed His prophet to inform the people that they had broken their relationship with Him. While they diligently carried out His command to fast, appearing to seek His mind, the Lord noted that they did so with the wrong motives. The people asked, "Why should we fast if You're not going to pay attention and hold up Your end of the bargain?" to which He responded,

Look, at the same time you fast, you satisfy your selfish desires, you oppress your workers. Look, your fasting is

214

accompanied by arguments, brawls, and fist fights. (Isaiah 58:3–4 NET)

According to God's thinking, a right relationship with Him will naturally result in a genuine love for others. My friend and colleague at Dallas Theological Seminary, Dr. Jeff Bingham, illustrated the principle this way: When a man marries a woman with children by a previous marriage, his vows are not to her alone. He cannot possibly love the woman without also loving the people she made.

The Lord declared that His people had blown it by mistreating one another. They allowed wrongs to remain unresolved and to grow, destroying their relationships in the process. As a result, their worship was tainted with hypocrisy.

To describe their sin and its oppressive results more specifically, He chose to use a farmer's yoke as a word picture. When I was stationed on Okinawa as a Marine, I saw farmers plowing their rice paddies walking behind great beasts—usually two oxen yoked together. A yoke is a custom-fitted, carved piece of thick timber that a farmer lays across an animal's shoulders, to which he connects chains or ropes in order to pull a plow.

In the case of the Hebrew, the yoke was laid across the shoulders of another person. One Hebrew reduced another Hebrew to the level of an ox—lower than a slave—exercising power or dominion over his brother or sister. Here's how the Lord identified the yoke: "You must remove the burdensome yoke from among you and stop pointing fingers and speaking sinfully" (Isaiah 58:9 NET).

The Hebrew word translated "sinfully" here has a wide range of meanings depending upon the context. It can mean "toil," "iniquity," or "deception," and in this case, probably all three simultaneously. The *Theological Wordbook of the Old Testament* adds this comment: "Generally, biblical theologians have given little attention to [this term] as a contributor to an understanding of sin. Since the word stresses the planning and expression of deception and points to the painful aftermath of sin, it should be noted more."[3]

"In the ancient world pointing the finger was involved in a formal accusation (as in Hammurabi's laws). The omen literature attaches to the gesture the power of a curse."[4] So it appears that wealthier Hebrews falsely accused their brothers and sisters in the courts in order to garnish their land and reduce them to indentured servanthood. Their false accusations placed a yoke on the shoulders of another.

Because no one can love the Lord without also loving the people He made, God demanded that they restore their relationships with each other. Isaiah 58:6–12 records His instructions to the people of Judah, from which we can derive at least five steps toward what I would call meaningful and successful reconciliation.

Step 1: Humble Yourself

The image of a yoke also symbolized the opposite of humility. The Lord wanted the oppressive Hebrew to destroy this implement of subservience. That would require him to humble himself. He would have to voluntarily approach those he had mistreated and release them from the burden he had laid upon them, which would require that he admit his fault and tell the truth. What's more, he would have to restore what he had taken and raise them up from their place of subservience to a level equal to or greater than his own importance.

> This is the kind of fast I want. I want you to remove the sinful chains, to tear away the ropes of the burdensome yoke, to set free the oppressed, and to break every burdensome yoke. (Isaiah 58:6)

According to the Lord, the first step to reconciliation was for the Hebrew to humble himself and make his sin right with his brother or sister. May I be painfully specific here? This is the willingness to say something like the following:

> I realize that I was wrong when I _____. As a result, I have allowed the distance between us to build. I have been wrong in my thinking and wrong in my words about you, and I have no excuse for my actions. I'm sorry I said and did those hurtful things. I will do what I can to restore what my actions took from you, but I acknowledge that nothing will completely erase the harm I have done. Will you please forgive me?

Recovering alcoholics like to say that humility is stark raving honesty. *Humble yourself.* Two simple words, yet how incredibly difficult! When I've had occasion to do this with our grown children (more than one), I have found that each of them met my decision to humble myself with astonishing compassion and kindness. I say this to their credit, but also to reveal the power of humility to open the way for reconciliation. I found them open and willing to hear me. They didn't disagree with my admissions of wrong, which were painful to accept but entirely appropriate. Nevertheless, I found each child eager for the offense to be cast into the deepest sea so that we could, again, enjoy our relationship without that awful, nagging, oppressive issue between us. Note the result in verse 6: "I want you to remove the sinful chains, to tear away the ropes of the burdensome yoke, *to set free the oppressed*" (emphasis added).

Your offense is their oppression. Set them free. Begin by humbling yourself.

Step 2: Pray

Remember, the passage began with the people fasting for selfish reasons. "Why have we fasted and You do not see? Why have we humbled ourselves and You do not notice?" The questions reveal their ignorance concerning God. The purpose of fasting in pagan religions was to get the gods to notice and heed the petitions of humans. With the Lord, the reason we fast is to help *us* hear *Him*. The purpose of prayer in the false religions of Canaan was to coerce the gods to release blessings and protection. For believers in the one true God, prayer is first and foremost a declaration of our dependence upon Him. We offer our supplications, but we submit our desires to Him because we trust in His ability to know what we need better than we do.

As for humility, the Lord isn't impressed by our ability to go without food. To Him, humility is regarding others as more important than self. And as long as we're not preoccupied with taking care of ourselves, we leave Him room to do it for us.

> Then your light will shine like the sunrise; your restoration
> will quickly arrive; your godly behavior will go before you,
> and the Lord's splendor will be your rear guard. Then you
> will call out, and the Lord will respond; you will cry out,
> and he will reply, "Here I am." (Isaiah 58:8–9 NET)

So before doing or saying anything, we must pray. We declare our dependence upon Him. We allow the Holy Spirit to change our hearts through the process of praying so that God informs us rather than the other way around. Again, I'll be specific. The prayer might go something like this:

> Lord, I feel awkward. I have erected so many barriers
> between us, and he has built a number of his own. Time
> has only deepened the hurt. I want to restore this relation-
> ship, but without Your help, Lord, my timing will be
> wrong, and I will say everything poorly. So I call upon You
> to help me discern the best time and express the right
> words.

When we determine to obey the Lord's commands, He promises to go before us and to watch our backs.

Step 3: Remove the Yoke

The yoke for the people of Judah was pointing the accusing finger and speaking evil. The restoration process depends upon our removing that yoke from our loved one. In an earlier chapter, I shared this insightful quote:

> Whenever we place blame, we are looking for a scapegoat for a real dislocation in which we ourselves are implicated. Blame is a defensive substitute for an honest examination of life that seeks personal growth in failure and self-knowledge in mistakes.[5]

I suggest you read that again, only more slowly and thoughtfully.

You know the adage "The best defense is a good offense." We protect ourselves when we put another down and engage in demagoguery. As long as we keep pointing the finger and casting blame, we can distract ourselves from the real problem. We are the ones who blew it.

Before you approach the person whom you have offended, drop all accusations. Prepare yourself by refusing to lay any blame at his or her feet. He or she may indeed own a lot of the responsibility for the strained relationship, but that is a matter for the Lord to resolve. Remove the yoke of blame and shame from the shoulders of the other and focus instead on yourself.

When you humble yourself, pray, and break the yoke, you'll be amazed by how well prepared you are for the fourth step.

Step 4: Make Yourself Available and Vulnerable

God required the people of Judah to remove the yoke from the shoulders of the oppressed only as a beginning. He wanted much more from them.

"You must actively help the hungry and feed the oppressed" (Isaiah 58:10 NET).

Restoring a relationship after we've blown it requires that we make ourselves vulnerable enough to acknowledge our wrong and accept the consequences . . . in person. In the award-winning film *Braveheart*, William Wallace's foolhardy action cost his father-in-law the life of his daughter. Without a word or hesitation, Wallace approached the man, handed him his own sword, and knelt before the grieving father with his neck exposed.

For the apology to be genuine, we must be willing to give the person we offended an opportunity to take his or her justice. We can ask for forgiveness, but we can't demand it or become resentful if the wounded person chooses retribution. Furthermore, our humility may require us to lower ourselves, to reverse roles with someone over whom we normally have authority, including one of our own children.

In addition to making ourselves vulnerable, we must make ourselves available to repair the damage we did and restore the health and happiness of the person we offended. This is not always in our ability; however, we need to offer to do what we can.

Before I discuss the final step, let me ask you some pointed questions in connection with that family member from whom you are estranged.

- Are you available to that family member who needs you? Is he or she aware of it?
- Do you make time to attend his or her events and meet his or her needs?
- Have you told this person that you miss him or her and you'd like to be closer?

I admit this puts you in a very vulnerable position. But as long as you remain in your defensive posture, you'll never make progress or begin the process of restoration. As long as you're worried about appearing foolish or weak, your relationships—not just this one, but all of them—will remain stagnant.

Step 5: Consider Yourself a Restorer

Not all relationships can be restored. Many—I dare say most—can, but not all. Sometimes the damage is so great that the other person can't or won't see past it. Sometimes the other person has a lot of other issues that make the hard work of reconciliation too difficult. Regardless, a victory has been won. Perhaps the other person didn't change and the relationship remains as cold and distant as before. Nevertheless, something did change.

> Then your light will rise in darkness
> And your gloom will become like midday.
> And the Lord will continually guide you,
> And satisfy your desire in scorched places,
> And give strength to your bones;
> And you will be like a watered garden,

And like a spring of water whose waters do not fail. Those
from among you will rebuild the ancient ruins; You will
raise up the age-old foundations;
And you will be called the repairer of the breach,
The restorer of the streets in which to dwell.
(Isaiah 58:10–12)

If we humble ourselves, pray, remove the yoke, and make
ourselves vulnerable and available, we will be utterly transformed. We have God's promise on it. Take note of the lush
imagery the Lord uses to describe the effect on Judah's people.
He pictures a dark, deserted wasteland suddenly flooded with
light and freshwater springs. Before long, the once-parched
land begins to buzz with commerce and family life. And in
time, the people gain a hero's reputation for building new cities
on old ruins.

Whether or not you are able to restore that broken relationship by stepping up and building your half of the bridge, you
legitimately can consider yourself "a restorer," a repairer of the
breach.

THREE ESSENTIALS IN THE
PROCESS OF RESTORATION

Experience has taught me three essential imperatives—three
"musts"—that propel a restorer forward. Disregard them, and
the process will almost certainly stall.

You must go with the right motive at the right time. This means
you approach the other person with no desire to manipulate his

or her emotions or gain pity for yourself. Your only purpose is to confess your wrong so he or she can heal. Take time to think about what you have done, think about what you have said, think about when the tension began. And when you have a fair understanding and have thought through your approach, then step up.

You must remain open and willing to hear whatever the other person has to say. In my experience, I've learned that this can be very difficult. You may not be completely aware of all the damage you have done. You thought your offense went only so deep, but it may have been much worse, which means you may be in for a lot more than you expected. In that situation, you may have to hear and absorb a lot of anger. The other person may become unreasonable and unload more than your fair share of the pain. Patiently endure. Hear all that for what it is: venting, not logic.

You must be patient. In the heat of the moment, remain calm and receive whatever the other person unloads and/or has to give. It may be immediate forgiveness or a long period of silent tension, or an intense eruption of anger. Whatever the response, resist the temptation to argue or make yourself understood. Set fairness aside in the interest of allowing him or her the space to be "unreasonable." Once the emotions have been spent, he or she will be able to think more clearly. (I often think of it as allowing someone to get rid of the bad feelings so there will be room for the good ones.)

In the meantime, wait. Allow the Lord to heal the wounds in His way, in His time. Very often the tension took years to build, so it won't be resolved in a one-hour session. Say what you need to say, then quietly and deliberately leave the situation in the Lord's hands.

~

As flawed, broken people, you and your mate will likely fail your children, which means you will have to take the lead in restoring the relationship. No family is immune to such challenges. My longtime friends Ann and Ray Ortlund had to do this with their son, Nels, many years ago. She writes in her book *Children are Wet Cement,*

> Only a few months ago Ray and I made a date with Nels and drove out into the hills overlooking Newport Beach.
>
> "Nels," said Ray, "I've goofed a lot as a dad. I love you very much, but I've said and done a lot of dumb things through your fifteen years. I know I've hurt and not helped lots of times, and I just want you to know that I'm sorry."
>
> There was a long silence. Nels didn't quite know how to respond.
>
> "Are you leading up to something?" he asked.
>
> "Not a thing," said Ray. "I just wanted to say that for all the times I've blundered and hurt you and done or said stupid things to you, to put you down or make life tougher for you, I really am sorry. I just wanted to apologize."
>
> I chimed in from the back seat of the car. "Nels, we didn't do dumb things on purpose; but we know we've been far from ideal parents. We've blown our tempers;

we've misjudged you; we haven't always handled you wisely—and that's been tough on you. We get intense and overzealous, overpicky on some issues, and we completely overlook other issues. We're just plain ol' dumb human beings. But our goofs have an influence on how you turn out—that's the scary part."

Ray said, "We think you're just turning out great. But whatever scars you've got, they're our fault, not yours. And don't think we don't realize that."

"That's okay," said Nels. "I think you're great."

"We sure are crazy about you, Nels," I said.

"We're proud of you," Ray added. "You're terrific—in spite of us."

"You're great parents," said Nels.

Over the seats of the car there were pats and smiles and squeezes.

That was it—pretty soon we drove down the hill and home again.[6]

Except in very rare cases, the person you have offended will love you more than ever for the effort you make in restoring that broken relationship. The process may be difficult and unpleasant, but the reward will be something that cannot be destroyed by fire or tragedy.

ELEVEN

When God's Gift Comes Specially Wrapped

hat we believe about God determines how we live our lives. Our theology affects everything about us: our decisions, our reactions to the circumstances of life, even how we will behave toward one another. This is true of everyone, even those who don't think they have a theological perspective. They may not have thought about their beliefs in a conscious, deliberate way, but their subconscious attitudes and decisions are anything but random. What we believe about God drives everything we think and do.

I have to admit that for many years I believed God to be *almost* sovereign in the universe, though I never would have admitted it. Of course, saying that God is almost sovereign is like saying someone is almost married or almost licensed to drive. Either one is or is not married, either licensed to drive or not. Sovereignty may have boundaries in terms of the realm in which a person rules, but within his or her sphere, sovereignty has no degrees. In other words, a sovereign king's earthly rule within his realm is absolute; he possesses supreme authority.

God is omnipresent, meaning that no place exists in which He is not present. He, therefore, has no boundaries or limits to His sovereignty. Furthermore, the Lord is omnipotent, meaning that nothing He chooses to do is beyond His ability. And He is omniscient, which means that He knows everything. He cannot learn and He cannot be taken by surprise.

When you put all of those truths together, you have to accept that nothing occurs that is beyond His control, apart from His command, or without His permission. Nothing. He rules over all events, including blessings and calamities. He rules over everything seen and unseen, material and immaterial, good and evil. No one can defeat His purposes or preclude His plans. From His perspective there are no mistakes and no accidents, even as they relate to pain, disease, and death.

Now, if the truth about God ended there, we would have every reason to be frightened of a rather cold, calculating, distant deity. After all, the world in which we live includes the existence of evil—sinful acts between people, as well as tragedies in nature. It is true that no evil occurs without God's sovereign permission; however, we must remember that this almighty God is also love and goodness and holiness and grace and mercy and compassion and patience and kindness. The very God who allows evil to continue on earth also subjected Himself to its terrible, destructive power along with us. The second member of the Godhead became a man in the person of Jesus Christ. And the God-man sealed the fate of evil by dying our death and rising again to offer us eternal life beyond the reach of sin and pain, sorrow and death.

While the Lord allows evil to continue, He has chosen to make the problem of pain His own. No one hates evil more than the Lord. Standing alongside the truth of God's sovereignty is His utterly holy, pure character. Holding one without the other will create an unbearable crisis of faith when we face difficulties. Now you can understand my opening sentence at the beginning for this chapter: what we believe about God determines how we live our lives. It drives everything we think and do.

Before going any further, let's be sure we're on the same page theologically. It may help for you to go back and reread those first three paragraphs.

TAKING GOD'S SOVEREIGNTY PERSONALLY

I'd like to probe your theology with a few questions. Is God sovereign if you lose your job due to no fault of your own? Is God sovereign when you practice longer and more diligently than anyone, yet someone else wins the competition? Is He sovereign when someone less qualified than you lands the promotion for which you worked and prayed so hard? Is He sovereign when a tornado rips your house from its foundation without taking so much as a shingle from the house next door? Is He sovereign when the spouse to whom you remained faithful and put through school runs off with a colleague shortly after graduation, leaving you with the children and the bills? Is He sovereign when a drunk driver slams into your car, leaving your child a quadriplegic? How about when all of the other babies in the hospital nursery are tagged "normal," while yours has an obvious birth defect? Is He sovereign over that situation?

I don't mind admitting a time in my ministry when I could not answer yes to all of those questions. And where I could answer in the affirmative, I was slow to speak. Fortunately, the Lord has developed my theology through the trials of real life so that now I can answer enthusiastically, "Yes! The Lord is absolutely, completely sovereign over all of those circumstances." I cannot say that I completely understand His ways nor can I explain why He does things the way He does. Nevertheless, I acknowledge His right to rule as He pleases and praise Him for His character. I have finally come to the place where I can accept His sovereign rule without feeling the need to understand or explain it.

SOVEREIGN OVER QUESTIONING

Centuries ago, the Lord confronted mankind on the issue of sovereignty. The prophet Isaiah faithfully recorded His words. Please read them slowly and thoughtfully.

> I am the LORD, and there is no other;
> Besides Me there is no God.
> I will gird you, though you have not known Me;
> That men may know from the rising to the setting of the
> sun
> That there is no one besides Me.
> I am the LORD, and there is no other,
> The One forming light and creating darkness,
> Causing well-being and creating calamity;
> I am the LORD who does all these.

Woe to the one who quarrels with his Maker—
An earthenware vessel among the vessels of earth!
Will the clay say to the potter, "What are you doing?"
Or the thing you are making say, "He has no hands"?
(Isaiah 45:5–7, 9)

Most of us don't have a problem accepting the consequences of our sin or our own bad decisions. After all, we're only getting what we deserve. But when calamity strikes out of nowhere due to no failing of our own, the flesh would have us tilt our faces toward heaven and shake our fists demanding to know why. Of course, mature Christians opt for a more reasonable approach. We present our case with cool, theological reasoning, and if that doesn't work, we bargain with Him.

On one occasion several months ago, Cynthia and I were wrestling with a particular affliction and could not make sense of it. After she went to bed, I stayed up late into the night looking for answers. I reminded the Lord of how many years I had faithfully served Him in ministry and how my conduct deserved better treatment. I paced the floor, saying, "Lord, I've faithfully served you, I've never run around on my wife, I've not stolen the church's money, I've never run off with the seminary's money (not that there's any to run away with, but we'll talk about that later), and I've always done my very best to be a good husband, father, pastor, and worshiper. How could You let this happen to me? This just isn't fair!"

Later, of course, I felt terribly stupid. And when I saw Isaiah 45:9, I shuddered a little. "Woe" is a Hebrew utterance that's not as much a word as it is a groan. It mimics the sound Jewish mourners made at funerals. "Woe to the one who quarrels with his Maker." The NET Bible renders that verse, "One who argues with his creator is in grave danger, one who is like a mere shard among the other shards on the ground!" I'm just thankful that our Maker is merciful.

He is the Potter; we are the clay. On His wheel, He does the shaping, He does the creating. He decides what clay will become a cup, or a bowl, or a pitcher. The clay doesn't shout back, "Hey! Watch it! Ouch, that hurts. No, not that. No!" With the Lord, no death is premature, though we see it that way. With the Lord, no diagnosis comes as a surprise, although we might be shocked. And with the Lord, there are no unexpected children or unwanted pregnancies. God never looks on a child as a mistake, nor does He regard any of them unfit, undesirable, substandard, or "defective."

We, as the clay, have no legitimate right to challenge the molding hands of the sovereign Potter.

SOVEREIGN THROUGH CREATION

Every child—every child—has been divinely formed to be a unique creation of the Father. And He makes no mistakes. King David celebrated the sovereign creation of the Lord in a song to be sung in the first person by all people.

For You formed my inward parts;
You wove me in my mother's womb.

I will give thanks to You, for I am fearfully and wonderfully
made;
Wonderful are Your works,
And my soul knows it very well.
My frame was not hidden from You,
When I was made in secret,
And skillfully wrought in the depths of the earth;
Your eyes have seen my unformed substance;
And in Your book were written all
The days that were ordained for me,
When as yet there was not one of them.
(Psalm 139:13–16)

This God-breathed hymn of praise affirms that the Lord's
creation includes no mistakes. No life is an afterthought to the
Lord. Every person arrives bearing the stamp "Made in Heaven
by the Sovereign Lord," which grants each child the dignity of
significance and purpose. The New Living Translation renders
Psalm 139:16, "You saw me before I was born. Every day of my
life was recorded in your book. Every moment was laid out
before a single day had passed."

The Hebrew word alternately translated "laid out" and
"ordained" is the same root word God used in Isaiah 45:9 when
He said, "Woe to the one who quarrels with His *Maker*." The
Maker has made the moments of our lives, and each moment
has a purpose. And nothing invalidates the destiny for which
we were created. Not gender, not nationality, not race, not even
what we often call "birth defects."

WHEN THE GIFT OF YOUR CHILD
COMES SPECIALLY WRAPPED

How easy to accept the truth of God's sovereign design when we gaze upon a cooing newborn and see ten fingers, ten toes, two beautiful eyes and ears, and perfectly formed arms, legs, and face. But how strong is our theology when that little gift from heaven comes specially wrapped? What about when we see obvious deformity, the heartrending sight of missing or contorted limbs, and distorted features? What happens to our notions of sovereign design, dignity, purpose, and destiny when we see the telltale signs of Down syndrome, spina bifida, or cleft palate? Let me push this to an extreme that nearly one out of a thousand new mothers face each year. What about the child afflicted with anencephaly, a missing or barely formed brain? How readily do we affirm that God has ordained the days—few as they are—for this little person?

My, how fragile our confidence in God's character! How quickly we discover the limits of our belief in His goodness!

I know for certain that God cherishes each life, and we can be sure that His plan includes those we would label "defective." I also know that God never wastes parents. Most new moms and dads dream of rearing the next Einstein, or Mozart, or the next Michael Jordan, and when their little one shows early signs of autism, they might be tempted to think that their child is inferior and their job is somehow less important. Profoundly autistic little boys and girls aren't likely to change the world on a grand scale (though there have been some remarkable exceptions.) However, like you and me, they do impact their part of it.

Michelle Schreder, a mother of two autistic children, writes,

What we need to learn as parents of children with special needs is how to enjoy this gift of life. This may seem impossible when we are waiting in yet another doctor's waiting room, cleaning out a feeding tube or changing another diaper on a child well past toddler stage. But the Giver of gifts makes no mistakes. He is life; and when we appreciate the life He has entrusted to us, we come to know Him and live in His life so much better.[1]

Special-needs children do impact the world, and their parents have a much more important job than they realize. Their children challenge our most basic system of values— those beliefs that shape our understanding of human esteem, worth, and acceptance. Each encounter with a disabled or mentally challenged child becomes a crisis of principles because they remind us that the kingdom of God looks at people from a very different perspective. Michelle Schreder continues,

We human beings constantly base a person's value and desirability on his or her looks, status, wealth, or accomplishments. . . . But clearly God does not. He welcomes everyone. . . . And He wants us, the people called by His name, to be a welcoming community as well.[2]

In one way or another and to different degrees, we are all uniquely challenged and we all need grace—the gift of complete acceptance and unqualified worth simply because God made us and values us. How important it is for us to thank God for children with special needs; without them, this comparison-obsessed world would soon have its way with our egos. And we must also thank God for the parents of these precious gifts, since these men and women are flesh-and-blood examples of the tender, unconditional, unrelenting love of God for all of us.

BIBLICAL ANSWERS TO DIFFICULT QUESTIONS

A carefully considered theology rarely ties up all the loose ends of reality. But it can provide realistic answers to tough questions. After all, theology apart from real life isn't much help. The most common questions I hear are variations of just three.

First, *did someone's sin cause my child's disability or abnormality?* The answer is complicated because it involves two very distinct issues that we frequently combine: the issues of consequences and divine punishment. Let me state this clearly: they are not the same. God is involved, but not the way we naturally think.

On the one hand, God almost always allows our actions to produce the expected consequences. Before we act, He instructs, He warns, and He frequently intervenes. He always puts us in the very best position to choose well and never allows us to be tempted beyond what we are able. Once we make our choice, however, He allows us to reap what we have sown. Using illicit drugs, abusing the use of alcohol, and smoking tobacco can damage a developing fetus, usually resulting in some kind of complication. Sins and poor choices usually produce unwanted consequences that can feel very much like punishment. However, these negative effects are not divine punishment, but divine grace. Reaping the unhappy fruit of what we have sown teaches us to be responsible managers of our own freedom. God, in His grace, uses the consequence of our sins and even the sins of the world to discipline and instruct us.

Divine punishment, on the other hand, is a very real product of sin; however, it does not come by way of natural consequences, but by supernatural wrath. It doesn't come indirectly through the world, but directly from God Himself. The arrival of Jesus Christ on earth began a new era, an age of grace. When Christ died on the cross, He took our sins upon Himself and endured the wrath of God on our behalf. If you have accepted His gift of grace by believing in Him, you will never experience the wrath—the divine punishment—you deserve. In grace, Jesus took it all and left *none* for you. None.

If, however, you choose to trust in your own goodness or hope that your good deeds will somehow purify or counteract your bad behavior, if you reject His free gift, God's wrath waits for you. When you die, or if the Lord should return before then, you will surely suffer divine punishment for your sins. But not before. Even though you continue to live in rebellion, the Lord uses the consequences of your sins and poor choices to teach you, all the while extending to you the offer of fellowship with Him.

God does not cause sin and He does not ordain evil. But He will use the sad results of sin and poor choices for His own purposes. When Jesus and His disciples encountered a man born blind—a congenital defect—He took the opportunity to clarify this very issue.

"As [Jesus] passed by, He saw a man blind from birth. And His disciples asked Him, 'Rabbi, who sinned, this man or his parents, that he would be born blind?'" (John 9:1–2)

A very few Jewish sects taught that a fetus could commit sins while a great many others held that disabilities in a newborn were the result of divine retribution against the parents. It's a natural question to ask if we don't know the character of God very well. I love Jesus's answer because it bypasses the question of punishment and goes right to the heart of the issue: trust in God's sovereignty and goodness.

"Jesus answered, 'It was neither that this man sinned, nor his parents; but it was so that the works of God might be displayed in him'" (John 9:3).

In my experience, no one more eloquently displays the works of God than the disabled, especially when they are children. Perhaps because children with disabilities make no apology for their need and willingly accept God's intervention in their lives—much more so than proud, arrogant, able-bodied adults. I've had a number of parents say to me, "I can't number the times that I've learned something profound about God and His work as a result of having a special-needs child. I've witnessed His patience; I've experienced His love and tenderness. I've discovered the power of dependence upon Him. I've embraced simple, childlike faith. I've been forced to be patient . . . to slow my pace and walk a little more carefully because of the time it takes to accommodate our child's needs. I have experienced life in ways I never would have otherwise."

Joni Eareckson Tada, a marvelous example to all of us, writes with clear-thinking honesty,

God doesn't just watch [harm] happen—he lets it happen. What is accidental from our perspective was specifically allowed by God. He who holds all things together must sustain the very molecules of the brick and axehead as they fly toward their mark (Colossians 3:17).

. . . Evil can only raise its head where God deliberately backs away—always for reasons that are specific, wise, and good, but often hidden during this present life. . . .

. . . God sees the evil already there and steers it to serve his good purposes and not merely Satan's viperous ones. It's as if he says, "So you want to sin? Go ahead—but I'll make sure you sin in a way that ultimately furthers my ends even while you're shaking your fist in my face." This is why we can accept troubles as ultimately from God even when the most dreadful people deliver them.[3]

As soon as Jesus finished correcting the theology of His disciples, He declared, "I am the light of the world" and then He gave the blind man sight. In this one act, Jesus demonstrated His authority over disabilities, sin, bad theology, the temple, the Sabbath, even the self-absorbed Pharisees who opposed Him. He had this opportunity because a little baby came into the world without the ability to see. God did not cause the baby's affliction; He gave it divine purpose before anything had been created.

A second question I often encounter: *How is God involved in birth defects and disabilities?*

We have established that the Lord is absolutely sovereign, yet He does not directly cause bad things to occur, such as physical and mental disabilities. However, they do occur by His permission, and He does directly ordain their purpose within His plan.

In Exodus 3–4, Moses stood before the burning bush arguing with God. He had spent his first forty years honing his natural abilities in Egypt, expecting to become the savior of Israel, perhaps by leading a military revolt against the Pharaoh. He saw an Egyptian abusing a Hebrew and took it upon himself to liberate his brother by murdering the attacker. He acted on his own initiative, in his own strength, expecting gratitude in return. Instead, the Lord remained silent, the Hebrew scoffed, and the Egyptian authorities sought his life.

Moses spent the next forty years of his life exiled, content to use his natural leadership skills on his father-in-law's flocks, resigning himself to the fact that he blew his big chance to rescue Israel. Then, at eighty years of age, he heard the Lord call to him. Standing barefoot before the eerie glow of God's presence, he heard the command, "Come now, and I will send you to Pharaoh, so that you may bring My people, the sons of Israel, out of Egypt" (Exodus 3:10). And so the argument began, during which we learn that Moses had a disability.

Moses first offered a number of reasons that God's plan wouldn't work, which the Lord countered by promising him miraculous abilities. After Moses exhausted all other excuses, he fell back to his last line of defense. "Master, please, I don't talk well. I've never been good with words, neither before nor after you spoke to me. I stutter and stammer" (Exodus 4:10 MSG). His actual words might have been, "I-I-I am s-s-s-s-slow of m-mouth aaaaand s-s-low of t-t-t-tongue." We forget that fact when we think of Moses, the leader of the Exodus. The man had a speech impediment, which he used as an excuse to keep from obeying God.

The Lord's response? Read it very carefully.

Who has made man's mouth? Or who makes him mute or deaf, or seeing or blind? Is it not I, the LORD? Now then go, and I, even I, will be with your mouth, and teach you what you are to say. (Exodus 4:11–12)

In other words, "Moses, you're talking to the Lord of mouths. Your disability is no surprise to Me, and it won't thwart My plans. In fact, your stammering tongue is part of My divine, sovereign strategy—always has been."

If your child was born blind, he or she was formed that way under the supervision of the Lord for His purposes and for His glory. It's not your fault; it's God's sovereign plan. Keeping this perspective can make all the difference for you and your child.

When I was a student at Dallas Theological Seminary, I got to know a very gifted young man a year or two behind me in his training. I remember thinking that his ability in the pulpit would give him a bright future in ministry. I have since lost touch with him but we enjoyed a nice friendship. I also remember that he had a birthmark that ran from his hairline, across his nose, down his cheek, jaw, and neck. It looked as though someone had dipped two fingers in bright, red paint and smeared it down his face. He intrigued me because he seemed to have no self-consciousness. His bold, confident presence revealed a security and even a sense of humor that few possess. One day I decided to come right out and ask him about it.

He smiled and said, "Actually, I have my dad to thank. For as long as I can remember, he used to say, 'Son, just before you were born that's where the angel kissed you. None of the other kids have that mark, and so that's how I know you're mine.'" He said, "You know, Chuck, it got to where I felt a little sorry for people who didn't have a red mark across their faces."

A third question I often hear: *If God is sovereign and hates evil, why would He allow this to happen to me, to us, to my family? Why does God wait to put an end to evil? Why does He not do it now?*

I find Paul's doxology in Romans 11 to be helpful. He raises his hands in praise and writes with much passion:

Oh, the depth of the riches both of the wisdom and knowledge of God! How unsearchable are His judgments and unfathomable His ways! For who has known the mind of the Lord, or who became His counselor? Or who has first given to Him that it might be paid back to him again? For from Him and through Him and to Him are all things. To Him be the glory forever. Amen. (Romans 11:33–36)

The answer to the third question is: *no one knows.* No one knows why God chooses as He does and acts as He does. Why one family's life would be marked by tragedy and another remains seemingly free of tragedy. Why disease and illness would nearly destroy one family while another stays healthy and strong. Or why the Lord doesn't come now to conquer the world and destroy evil and remove disabilities forever.

If I were able to answer these three questions with complete satisfaction, we would have other questions to take their place. At some point, even the most brilliant and accomplished theological minds must cast aside their books and notes to praise the Lord. And they choose to praise Him for His character in the absence of tidy resolutions. To this last question and a hundred more like it, I openly admit, "I don't know." But where my knowledge fails, I can trust the Lord's sovereignty and goodness, ultimately, to make everything right.

Perspectives

I began this chapter with the bold claim that our theology affects everything about us—our decisions, how we will react to the circumstances of life, even how we will behave toward one another. Right thinking demands right action.

TO THOSE WHO HAVE SPECIAL-NEEDS CHILDREN

I want to be very, very careful as I write this because I am not a parent of a disabled child, though I am a grandfather of one. My wife and I have watched as our daughter and son-in-law endure the sadness, heartache, frustration, and sheer exhaustion of rearing an autistic son. So my experience as a grandparent qualifies me to sympathize with better-than-average knowledge, but I cannot offer firsthand advice.

To you, I hope you will trust God each day for new strength. I hope you will not hesitate to admit your weakness, to allow yourself frustration and sadness, and to request the help of others often. In many ways, the job requires superhuman energy, superhuman patience, and superhuman diligence and wisdom. And because you generally get the job done fairly well, you can easily forget that you're only human.

TO THOSE WHO DO NOT HAVE SPECIAL-NEEDS CHILDREN

Let's reach out, even if we don't know how or don't know what to say.

I notice that people who encounter those who are disabled tend either to stare uncompassionately from a distance or ignore them completely. Very few people talk to disabled people or the people helping them or even their parents. And I understand why. We're afraid of offending or saying something that will embarrass either ourselves or the other person. For example, in a church where I formerly served, I happened to be standing nearby when a woman pushing her husband in a wheelchair approached an usher for a worship folder. The usher held out a folder and said, "Good morning. This is for you. Does he want one?"

She very politely replied, "Why don't you ask him?"

Of course, the embarrassed usher—a fine, sensitive gentleman—was mortified over his thoughtless question. After he confirmed that the husband wanted one and saw the couple to their seat, he wanted to crawl into a hole somewhere on the dark side of the moon.

No one wants to offend or feel embarrassed, but the encounter was better than the alternative. He risked and blundered . . . and learned. For all its awkwardness, it involved an authentic human interaction that disabled people often crave. For sure, next time, that usher will know to look in those eyes and address a person in a wheelchair directly.

Let me encourage you to reach out. Engage. Risk saying or doing the wrong thing. Begin by treating a disabled person as you would any other person, then as you observe or as he or she directs, adjust to accommodate the disability. If you goof, apologize and accept his or her grace. Judging by the conversations I've had, they much prefer your well-intentioned efforts to being ignored.

May I be bold here? *We are all disabled.* Some disabilities are more difficult to hide than others, and most of us do a great job keeping our disabilities safely concealed (which is a major problem!). But we all have special needs. Thankfully, we have a Savior who looks directly at each one of us, seeing us as we are and valuing us as His own prized creation.

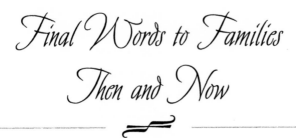

TWELVE

Final Words to Families Then and Now

$\mathcal{W}$riting the last chapter of a book comes with mixed emotions. I usually feel a sense of gratitude for all that I learned personally and for the opportunity to share what I learned with you. And, of course, I feel accomplishment having completed this literary journey. Admittedly, there is also great relief in finishing a project this extensive. In my reading, I came across Winston Churchill's description of the painstaking process of writing a book:

> Writing a book is an adventure. To begin with it is a toy, an amusement; then it becomes a mistress, and then a master, and then a tyrant and then the last phase is that, just as one is about to be reconciled to one's servitude, one kills the monster.[1]

As I prepare this monster, my mind retraces the steps we've taken together along our journey.

We discovered from the wisdom of Proverbs the best-kept

secret of wise parenting: "Cultivate a thirst, initiate a hunger, create an appetite for spiritual things in the lives of children of any age, as long as they are living under your roof, and do it in keeping with the way they are bent—disciplining the disobedience and dealing with the evil while affirming and encouraging the good, the artistic, the beautiful. As children begin to grow into adults, their paths will be aimed directly toward the Savior, and they will continue to walk in His sovereignty."

We allowed Scripture to show us that children are bent in two conflicting ways. Each child was created by God to be good and to fulfill His purpose for him or her; yet, from the moment of conception, sin has corrupted the nature of each child so that he or she rejects God's way for foolishness. The rod and reproof are the parents' tools to curb the natural, stubborn, rebellious impulses of children in order to teach them self-control and to guide them toward the Savior.

We thought about how to train and nourish children without indulging them, how to discipline without crushing their spirits, and how to shape their wills without draining their enthusiasm for life. We considered the sad occasion when children exercise their own wills and choose to walk away from the values and principles we taught them to honor. We examined the grace-giving heart of the father in Jesus's story of two rebel sons. We looked in on a strong, godly family to appreciate the value of children and their priority over career advancement or personal fulfillment. And we rediscovered the beauty of God's design and the security of His sovereignty in the gift of children who come to us specially wrapped.

It's been quite a journey. This is a good time to pause for some final reflections.

FINAL WORDS TO FAMILIES

The book of Deuteronomy forms a final chapter in the journey of Moses. It is here the travel-weary leader does what I'd like to do: he pauses, ponders where they had been, and then draws out some helpful insights to be remembered. At the age of one hundred and twenty, he had led the Israelites out of captivity in Egypt and cared for them during their forty-year sojourn in the desert, yet "his eye was not dim, nor his vigor abated" (Deuteronomy 34:7); he had snow on his roof, but he still had fire in his furnace. The venerable old man was still strong, still able to meet the challenges of life, but his journey had come to an end. The Lord told His servant that it was time for him to come on home. Accepting God's decision to close his books, Moses delivered his last series of messages to the Hebrew nation in which he reiterated the Lord's commands. This restatement and review of the Law in the book titled Deuteronomy is a Greek term that means "second law."

Israel stood on the threshold of the Promised Land for the second time. The first generation had failed to enter the land forty years earlier because they feared their enemies more than they trusted their Lord. This new generation was to receive the long-awaited Promised Land, and Moses wanted to be sure they would not fail to obey Him as they claimed the blessings God prepared for them. Keep in mind that Canaan, the land they were to inhabit, was filled with idol-worshiping pagans whose influence and lifestyle saturated every square foot of ground and permeated the walls of every structure.

The last words of Moses sound like a speech a father might give a son or daughter getting ready to leave for college. His favorite word throughout Deuteronomy is "remember," as if to say, "Now don't forget . . . Keep this in mind . . ."

Deuteronomy 6 records what is perhaps his most important message. Throughout the three millennia since Moses first delivered these words up to the present day, the Hebrew people consider this passage their confession of faith. They call it the "Shema," a name derived from the Hebrew term forming the opening command, "Hear!" or "Listen!"

"Hear, O Israel! The LORD is our God, the LORD is one!" (Deuteronomy 6:4).

The people of the one true God would enter a land of many false gods. They would inhabit cities they didn't establish, live in homes they didn't build, drink from wells they didn't dig, and eat from groves and vineyards they didn't plant. All this unexpected and instant affluence would present a new kind of danger.

Imagine suddenly inheriting a vast fortune or winning a $100 million lottery, and moving among the cultural elite. In all the excitement and affluence, there would be a great temptation to forget our dependence upon the Lord and grow indifferent to Him. To prevent this, the Lord commanded His people through Moses,

"You shall bind [these words] as a sign on your hand and they shall be as frontals on your forehead" (Deuteronomy 6:8).

At some point in Jewish history, worshipers took this

command literally, and to this day, orthodox and conservative Jews wear two leather pouches during morning prayers: one on the forehead, the other on the right hand. Tucked inside are little strips of parchment printed with the text of important passages of Scripture. Similarly, almost every home and business in Israel has taken Deuteronomy 6:9 just as literally: "You shall write them on the doorposts of your house and on your gates." Jews customarily affix a little tube called a mezuzah (Hebrew for "doorpost") to the doorpost of their homes, offices, even hotel rooms, sometimes placing the sacred words of Scripture inside.

Cynthia and I brought a silver mezuzah back from Israel, and we plan to secure it on the front doorpost of the house we've built in Frisco, Texas. This will be our way of giving tangible expression to our devotion. It will also remind us, as it did that ancient generation of God-worshipers about to face the challenges of prosperity, that we belong to the Lord and everything we are and have is from Him. We are living in a house that He allowed us to build. We eat food from His hand, and we drink water that He has provided for us. We enjoy the protection and provision of the Almighty. Even the joy and the laughter that echo from our walls are a testimony to His immeasurable grace to us as a couple and to our entire extended family.

SIX PRINCIPLES FOR OUR GOOD AND FOR OUR SURVIVAL

God's promises to us are not conditional. However, "our good and our survival" most definitely have conditions. A mezuzah in no way guarantees our obedience. We can choose to forget Him, forsake His commandments, ignore His warnings, and allow our prosperity and pagan influences to woo us away from dependence upon the Lord, but we do so at our own peril. Those He has called, He has saved; and He will preserve those He has saved to the end. However, He has given us a large stake in determining the quality of our own lives and of the little people He has given us to steward. He has given us the power to influence the environment in which we rear our children and to choose the legacy we pass on to them. That's why the Lord directed Moses to deliver these final messages.

I want to end our journey by having us pause and reflect on what many consider to be Moses's most important speech. I find in Deuteronomy 6:4–25 six principles that the Lord intended for the Israelites—and us—to follow "for our good always and for our survival" (v. 24). Please do not rush through this last chapter. Take your time. Ponder each principle slowly and carefully since they are timeless and true.

Principle 1: Parents Cannot Pass Along What They Themselves Do Not Possess

> Hear, O Israel! The LORD is our God, the LORD is one! You shall love the LORD your God with all your heart and with all your soul and with all your might. These words, which I am commanding you today, shall be on your heart. (Deuteronomy 6:4–6)

God is pleading for passion here. He wants us to put our whole hearts into our relationships with Him! Dr. Clyde Cook, president of Biola University, once told me about an unusual sight he and his wife, Anna Belle, saw on their visit to Sea World. They explored the aquariums, watched Shamu soak spectators, and marveled as the sea lions and walruses played catch. At one point, they were strolling down a big walkway when about a dozen ducks—all on roller skates—sort of scooted and shuffled their way toward them. I said, "That must have been a funny sight. Roller-skating ducks."

He replied, "The closer they got to us, the more obvious it became that they could do it, but I could tell they didn't have their hearts in it."

Cynthia and I now have an expression we use on occasion: "He's a duck on roller skates." That describes someone going through the motions, even making a little progress, but you can tell he doesn't have his whole heart in it.

I notice that the command isn't merely, "Believe in God, go to church, read your Bible, sing the songs, and pray at mealtime." No, we are to love the Lord "with *all* . . . and with *all* . . . and with *all* . . ." Children can tell when we're just going through empty, religious motions. Halfhearted devotion is as obvious—and just as unnatural—as a duck on roller skates. Kids are ruthlessly insightful and painfully honest. They want to know what works. They don't want to waste their time believing in something that doesn't make sense or won't have a significant impact on their lives. And if they see you giving the Lord the scraps of your time, your money, and your energy, what are they to conclude? Only that love for the Lord can be compromised without consequence.

We cannot pass on what we do not personally possess. A phony faith won't cut it, which prompts the next principle.

Principle 2: Children Won't Benefit from What Isn't Authentic

> You shall teach them diligently to your sons and shall talk of them when you sit in your house and when you walk by the way and when you lie down and when you rise up. (Deuteronomy 6:7)

Take note of where and when the training should take place. There's not a word about church services, nothing about the Hebrews' Sabbath or their festivals or sacrifices. Nothing here about religion at all. Love for the Lord and His Word have virtually nothing to do with religion. Christianity is a relationship, not a body of knowledge or a system of thought, and it has absolutely no place for "churchianity." There's nothing wrong with church. I preach sermons almost every Sunday of my life in one. But if we're not careful, we can check all authenticity at the door, put on a church mask, spout church vocabulary, and lose the very quality that made Christ so attractive to sinners . . . and children.

The Hebrew term translated "diligently" in Deuteronomy 6:7 comes from the verb "to sharpen." And when Moses wrote this, he used an intensive form of the verb. This is not to suggest that our teaching needs to be like boot camp, but that it is to be consistent and should take place in every segment of our lives. Your children need to see your love for the Lord in the grocery store, and in line at the post office, and in the snarl of traffic . . . in every, ordinary aspect of life. Take authenticity out of Christianity, and all you have is religious-looking rituals without heart. You have nothing of any practical value for facing challenges that ruin lives. The challenges we face don't come in the form of multiple-choice Bible quizzes. They test our character. They prove the genuineness of our belief, the reality of our relationship with God. And our children are watching. And may I add something convicting? They take their cues from our examples. They *will* do as we have done!

Shortly before her death, television comedienne Gilda Radner wrote a poignant little book titled *It's Always Something*, in which she told this story:

> When I was little, Dibby's cousin had a dog, just a mutt, and the dog was pregnant. I don't know how long dogs are pregnant, but she was due to have her puppies in about a week. She was out in the yard one day and got in the way of the lawn mower, and her two hind legs got cut off. They rushed her to the vet and he said, "I can sew her up, or you can put her to sleep if you want, but the puppies are okay. She'll be able to deliver the puppies."
>
> Dibby's cousin said, "Keep her alive."
>
> So the vet sewed up her backside and over the next week the dog learned to walk. She didn't spend any time worrying, she just learned to walk by taking two steps in

the front and flipping up her backside, and then taking two steps and flipping up her backside again. She gave birth to six little puppies, all in perfect health. She nursed them and then weaned them. And when they learned to walk, they all walked like her.[2]

Children have the amazing ability to bypass what we say and even what we *think* we believe and they zero in on what our *actions* model we believe. They won't benefit from a love for the Lord that isn't authentic. Stay real, parents!

Principle 3: Truth Isn't a Core Commitment if It Lacks Courageous Convictions

> You shall bind them as a sign on your hand and they shall be as frontals on your forehead. You shall write them on the doorposts of your house and on your gates. (Deuteronomy 6:8–9)

Wearing the Lord's words on our hand and forehead not only reminds us of our devotion, but it also declares to a watching world that we belong to God. To the Israelites entering the Promised Land, He said, in effect, "When you claim the land of Canaan and you're enjoying your newfound prosperity, and before you have successfully driven out the pagan influence I have asked you to expel, your faith will be challenged. I want them to know from the start that you belong to Me. Wear My words on your head, strap them to your hand, and write them on your doors and gates. Make My Word your public declaration."

Let's face it; most of us want to be liked more than we want to be upright. When you're all alone at a PTA meeting and a moral principle's at stake, it's tough to stand up and give voice to the truth of Scripture. When you're on the job and your organization wants to compromise standards or bend ethical rules, taking the moral high road can cut a career short. Speaking up might label you as someone who's not a team player. Those moments of truth tend to clarify one's core commitments. Genuine core commitments don't crumble under pressure. In fact, they usually grow stronger.

I first met Dr. Chuck McElhenney many years ago during an intern trip. He lived and ministered at First Orthodox Presbyterian Church in the Sunset District of San Francisco, an area known to be hostile to Christians due to radical homosexuals and lesbians. His house had been firebombed, his church invaded and graffitied more times than he could count, and his ministry marched against and protested regularly. When I traveled to meet him, I expected to find him wearing a steel helmet shouldering a shotgun, huddled in a house with barred windows, surrounded by a couple of snarling rottweilers. I envisioned this guy locked in a perpetual battle with evil, slugging it out with those who would love to see him destroyed or at least discouraged. Instead, I found a man who deeply loved the people who hated him so much. He ministered there for more than twenty-five years, preaching the gospel and loving the people God brought his way. Now much of his ministry takes place in hospitals, tending the needs of people dying of AIDS.

Though his ministry didn't center on politics, one morning he read in the *San Francisco Chronicle* about a proposal by the city council that went too far. Rather than sit back and keep his mouth shut, he decided to attend a hearing on the council's resolution. When the council opened the microphone to the floor, my friend decided to make a case for the biblical approach to the matter. In the most eloquent, gracious, and intelligent manner, he exposed the flaws in the resolution the council was about to pass. Without naming them, he was careful to weave the words of Moses, Paul, and David into his presentation, which the panel found compelling. Just as he was about to return to his seat, a council member spoke up and asked, "Sir, were those quotes in your presentation taken from the Bible?"

He calmly affirmed that his reasoning and many of his words were taken directly from Scripture. And with that, the council member said, "Well, if that's in the Bible, then I vote no." He changed his vote to strike down the resolution. That council member's statement gave others courage enough to vote with him. In the end, the resolution failed to pass, just as Chuck had hoped.

This example represents more of the exception than the rule. Rarely does the choice to exercise courage cause such a dramatic shift. But the Lord didn't call us to change the world from a huge public platform, only to be faithful to Him on a day-to-day basis. What happens after we live and proclaim the truth is His responsibility.

Dr. John Walvoord, the longtime president and chancellor emeritus at Dallas Theological Seminary, challenged our graduating class back in 1963 with a statement I have never forgotten. He said, "My fear is that we may be graduating individuals having too many beliefs but not enough convictions."

It's not enough that we know the truth; we must live the truth with courageous conviction for it to mean anything to others, including our children.

Principle 4: Prosperity Without Personal Sacrifice Often Leads to Indifference Toward God

> Then it shall come about when the LORD your God brings you into the land which He swore to your fathers, Abraham, Isaac and Jacob, to give you, great and splendid cities which you did not build, and houses full of all good things which you did not fill, and hewn cisterns which you did not dig, vineyards and olive trees which you did not plant, and you eat and are satisfied, then watch yourself, that you do not forget the LORD who brought you from the land of Egypt, out of the house of slavery. (Deuteronomy 6:10–12)

I once heard an intriguing claim. I don't know how true it is, but it sounds plausible. If you eat three meals each day, have five changes of clothing in your closet, live in a dwelling equipped with indoor plumbing and air conditioning, and own an automobile, you are among the top 5 percent of the world's wealthiest people. In light of that statement, chances are good that the word *affluent* describes you. Technology alone has provided us with luxuries our grandparents could only have imagined.

Please get this straight: there is nothing wrong with being

blessed. No one should feel guilty for having nice things. However, there is danger in prosperity that we did not earn— wealth that came to us apart from personal sacrifice. The inherent danger is spiritual indifference. We can too easily turn our eyes from the Giver to the gift and thereby weaken trust in Him. Soon we will look to our prosperity for our safety, for our identity, for our significance, all of which give rise to a spirit of entitlement.

This has particular relevance for our children. For much of their lives, they live in homes nicer than their parents were reared in, have money in their pockets they didn't earn, play games on a computer they didn't buy, drive cars nicer than their parents drove for which they have no monthly payment, and wear clothes and eat food obtained through their parents' earn- ings. When we think about that, Moses's warning makes a lot of sense: "Watch out!" And so we must warn our children.

Gary Bauer adds these insightful observations:

What most parents probably don't appreciate is how sophisticated and exact a science marketing to children has become. If God knows when every sparrow falls and the number of hairs on every man's head, the merchants of Hollywood and Wall Street know how many coins jingle in a child's pocket . . . and how to get them.

A recent article in *American Demographics*, a monthly magazine charting trends of interest in the U.S. business, discussed the "littlest shoppers," and the steps industry can take to attract the purchasing power of children, both the money they spend directly and the parental spending they influence. The article estimated that child influenced expenditures in the United States total $132 billion annually.[3]

These statistics are twelve years old, yet the trend hasn't slowed as far as I can determine. I recently drove to a high school to take one of our grandchildren to lunch and found no place to park. The parking lot looked like a new car dealership. Most of the vehicles were *far* more expensive than my pickup truck.

Again, I'm not suggesting that parents should withhold nice things from their children. Cynthia and I have delighted to give our four kids the best we could afford. We want them to enjoy our abundance *before* we're gone. We want to see them benefit from God's blessing on us now! But never at the expense of their relationship with the Lord. As you give to your children, help them cultivate a heart of thanksgiving. Always point them to the provision and protection of the Lord, the true source of all that's good. Remind them often of God's great grace . . . and also His holiness.

Principle 5: Compromising Faith in the One True God Is Politically Correct but Spiritually Lethal

You shall fear only the LORD your God; and you shall worship Him and swear by His name. You shall not follow other gods, any of the gods of the peoples who surround you, for the LORD your God in the midst of you is a jealous God; otherwise the anger of the LORD your God will be kindled against you, and He will wipe you off the face of the earth. (Deuteronomy 6:13–15)

We live during a time when all gods claim to point to the same being, when sincerity is the primary concern, when the only belief unworthy of tolerance is an exclusive one. *Merriam-Webster's Collegiate Dictionary* defines *tolerance* as "sympathy or indulgence for beliefs or practices differing from or conflicting with one's own; the act of allowing something."[4]

Tolerance has been the keystone of religious freedom in America, and it rests on the notion that each individual must answer to God for himself or herself. However, many in our day would redefine *tolerance* to mean that we must *accept* another's belief as equally true as our own, not merely *allow* another to believe as he or she chooses. As Josh McDowell points out in his book *The New Tolerance*, failure to give other beliefs and other gods equal standing with the God of the Bible may earn the labels, bigot, narrow-minded," or the ultimate insult, intolerant." When tolerance becomes concession, we have compromised our faith leading to a certain spiritual demise. Our culture is pervasive and persuasive—our kids and grandkids are exposed to it every day. They need our help in learning how to keep thinking straight in a world that's lost its way.

The Canaanites were not only pagan in their beliefs, but they were remarkably inclusive. They would generally accept any god they thought might improve their crops or protect their borders. The Lord, however, expected complete, undivided devotion from His people. Take note of the exclusive language used by Moses.

One very respected lexicon has this to say about the term translated "jealous":

> This verb expresses a very strong emotion whereby some quality or possession of the object is desired by the subject. ... It may prove helpful to think of "zeal" as the original sense from which derived the notions "zeal for another's property" ="envy" and "zeal for one's own property" = "jealousy."[5]

We have to be careful how we apply this. The Lord can be zealous about the truth of His claim on our lives, and He has the right to be forceful about it. As the perfect judge, He has prerogative that we don't. I'm embarrassed to see fellow believers condescending, condemning, pointing fingers, and being entirely unkind—even rude—to people who do not worship our God. We can devote ourselves to the one true God, and we can refuse to compromise our faith in attractive, winsome ways if we choose. The late Reinhold Niebuhr put it well:

> You may be able to compel people to maintain certain minimum standards by stressing duty, but the highest moral and spiritual achievements depend not upon a push but a pull. People must be charmed into righteousness.[6]

We could take a lesson from the apostle Paul. No one could ever accuse that strong-hearted apostle of compromise. If anything, he gained a reputation for staunch convictions and straight talk. Nevertheless, he greeted the pagan philosophers of Athens with an affirmation. While waiting for Silas and Timothy to join him, "his spirit was being provoked within him as he was observing the city full of idols" (Acts 17:16). Soon he found himself on Mars Hill, surrounded by the city's most influential minds—brilliant minds, yet twisted and darkened by idolatry. He began his address with gracious words, "Men of Athens, I observe that you are very religious in all respects" (Acts 17:22). And from there, he began to tell them of Jesus Christ, the God-man who rose from the dead. Most rejected him. A few believed that day and became his students.

Our responsibility is not to be popular or accepted, but to speak the truth. Yet we need not be offensive in the process. Our duty is to worship the one true God exclusively and without apology. Yet we need not be ugly or arrogant about it. If we speak the truth in love and live out our devotion with humility, we will not only provide the lost an attractive "pull" toward the Lord, but we'll also prepare our children to resist the inevitable temptation to compromise their faith. It's a delicate balance, but it's well worth the effort.

Principle 6: Mercy Brought Us Out, Grace Brings Us In, but Obedience Enables Us to Survive

> He brought us out from [Egypt] in order to bring us in, to give us the land which He had sworn to our fathers. So the Lord commanded us to observe all these statutes, to fear the Lord our God for our good always and for our survival, as it is today. (Deuteronomy 6:23–24)

The connection between the institution of family and obedience to God could not be clearer. In establishing the terms of the old covenant, the Lord placed great value on the family as a means to perpetuate worship and devotion to Him and, thus, to preserve the nation (Deuteronomy 6:20–21). And the connection worked both ways. He promised that obedience would prolong the days of each generation and that He would heap blessing upon blessing (Deuteronomy 7:12–13).

Today, in this era of grace, we enjoy a different arrangement. We no longer live under the conditional blessings and curses of the Mosaic Covenant. Jesus Christ satisfied the conditions of that old covenant and superseded it with a new one. However, we share several things in common with the ancient Hebrew people.

First, *we have been given a great gift by the grace of God.* Those who have placed their faith in Jesus Christ have been brought out of slavery to sin and, by grace, have been brought into fellowship with the Father. This personal relationship with the living God is our Promised Land; nothing and no one can take it from us. It is God's unconditional gift to His children.

Second, *affluence and rival systems of thought threaten to distract us from single-minded devotion to the Lord.* We too easily overlook our complete dependence upon God. Like the Israelites, I repeat, we must "watch out!"

And finally, *our relationship with God is secure, but our adversary wants nothing more than to see our destruction.* Once we are in Christ, Satan cannot have our souls, but he can make our lives miserable. Obedience to the Lord is our way of participating in and cooperating with the Lord's desire to see "our good always and our survival."

Deuteronomy 6 in Three Movements

If we step back from Deuteronomy 6 in order to view it as a whole, I see a diagram of our lives as three concentric circles. Each circle can represent the investment of whatever we might have: our time, our money, our concerns, our energy, priorities, thoughts, love . . . you name it. In the center, at the very core of everything is *the Lord.* "You shall love the LORD your God." The Lord must be the first recipient of all are and all you own. Anything you invest with Him will naturally benefit others in your life. And as a parent, this primary responsibility will keep your heart soft.

The next circle, radiating outward from the core, is *family.* "You shall teach [these words] diligently to your sons." Taking good care of your family will help keep your priorities straight. This will require authenticity and vulnerability with each member, including the youngest. On many occasions, I have found the innocent remarks of a little one to be just the rebuke I needed. Allow the Lord to keep your heart soft, remain sensitive to the needs of your family, and each decision you must make will become remarkably clear.

The third circle represents *friends, the workplace, church, and community.* "You shall bind [these words] as a sign." Everyone you meet should eventually discover that you live by the Word of God. Not because you carry a Bible wherever you go, but because they see you living peacefully and graciously with others. When you live in such harmony with others, your relationships will grow increasingly close, deep, and strong.

Love the Lord.

Take good care of your family.

Live peacefully with others.

Almost everything else Moses would say to the families of Israel was an exposition of these three commands. May we take heed.

Why? Because it's "for our good" and because it will result in "our survival."

I mean it with all my heart when I write this: my prayers and my thoughts are with you as you stay at the tasks of parenting. Looking back over many, many years, I can assure you, it is worth *all* the effort!

Notes

Introduction

1. "Would You Have Kids Again?" from Ann Landers column, © Creators Syndicate. Used by permission. All rights reserved.

Chapter 1

1. Francis F. Brown, S. R. Drive, and Charles A. Briggs, *The Brown-Driver-Briggs Hebrew and English Lexicon* (Peabody, Mass.: Hendrickson Publishers, Inc., 2000), 335.
2. Brown, 335.
3. Ibid.
4. Don Parker, *Using Biblical Hebrew in Ministry: A Practical Guide for Pastors, Seminarians, and Bible Students* (New York: University Press of America, 1995), 143.
5. Biblical Studies Press, The NET Bible Notes, Pr. 22:6, text note 16, Biblical Studies Press, 2003.
6. Reprinted from *You've Got to Be Kidding.* Copyright © 2004 by Pat and Ruth Williams. Used by permission of WaterBrook Press, Colorado Springs, CO. All rights reserved.

Chapter 2

1. Charlie Shedd, *Promises to Peter* (Waco, Tex.: Word Books, Inc. 1970), 7.
2. James Swanson. *Dictionary of Biblical Languages with Semantic Domains: Hebrew (Old Testament).* Electronic ed., HGK222. Oak Harbor: Logos Research Systems, Inc. 1997.
3. R. Laird Harris, Gleason L. Archer, Jr., and Bruce K. Waltke, eds., *Theological Wordbook of the Old Testament,* Vol. (Chicago: Moody, 1999), 467.
4. Harris, 650.
5. Biblical Studies Press, The NET Bible Notes, Psalm 51:5, Biblical Studies Press, 2003.
6. James Dobson, *Straight Talk to Men and Their Wives* (Sisters, Ore.: Multnomah, 1998), 58–60.
7. Harris, 440.

Chapter 3

1. Charles Bridges, *A Commentary on Proverbs* (Edinburgh: Banner of Truth Trust, 1974), 413.
2. W. E. Vine, Merrill F. Unger, and William White, *Vine's Complete Expository Dictionary of Old and New Testament Words* (Nashville: Thomas Nelson, 1996), 1:164.

3. R. Laird Harris, Gleason L. Archer, Jr., and Bruce K. Waltke, eds., *Theological Wordbook of the Old Testament*, Vol. (Chicago: Moody, 1999), 651.

4. Dr. James Dobson, *The New Strong-willed Child: Birth through Adolescence* (Wheaton, Ill.: Tyndale House Publishers, 2004), 57.

Chapter 4

1. Charles Norman, e. e. cummings: *The Magic Maker* (New York: Little, Brown & Co., 1973), 353.

2. Charles R. Swindoll, *Come Before Winter...and Share My Hope* (Sisters, Ore.: Multnomah, 1985), 83.

3. Pablo Casals, "You Are a Marvel" from *Chicken Soup for the Soul*, edited by Jack Canfield and Mark Victor Hansen. Copyright © 1992 by Jack Canfield and Mark Victor Hansen. Reprinted with the permission of Health Communications, Inc., www.hcibooks.com.

4. William Barclay, *The Letter to the Galatians* (Lewisville, Ken.: Westminster John Knox Press, 2002), 211-212.

5. James Dobson, *Bringing Up Boys* (Wheaton, Ill.: Tyndale, 2001), 35–36.

6. David Seamands, *Healing for Damaged Emotions* (Colorado Springs: Victor Books, a division of Cook Communications, 1981), 49.

7. Brennan Manning, *Abba's Child* (Colorado Springs: NavPress, 2002), 34.

8. James Dobson, *Hide or Seek* (Grand Rapids, Mich.: Fleming Revell, a division of Baker Books, 2001), 146.

9. Tim Kimmel, *Why Christian Kids Rebel* (Nashville: Thomas Nelson, 2004), 108–109. Used by permission of Thomas Nelson, Inc. All rights reserved.

10. Kimmel, 133.

Chapter 5

1. Alexander Whyte, *Bible Characters* (London: Oliphants Ltd., 1952), 1:309.

2. Ibid.

3. Cornelius Tactius, *The Life of Gnaeus Julius* (G. Dearborn, 1836), 42:15.

4. Biblical Studies Press, The NET Bible Notes, 2 Samuel 13:21, Biblical Studies Press, 2003.

5. Tim Kimmel, *Why Christian Kids Rebel* (Nashville: Thomas Nelson, 2004), 214. Used by permission of Thomas Nelson, Inc. All rights reserved.

Chapter 6

1. Alexander Whyte, *Bible Characters* (London: Oliphants Ltd., 1952), 1:309.

2. James Dobson, *Bringing Up Boys* (Wheaton, Ill.: Tyndale, 2001), 35–36.

3. Taken from *Parents in Pain* by John White. Copyright © 1979 InterVarsity Christian Fellowship of the USA. Used with permission of InterVarsity Press, PO Box 1400, Downers Grove, IL 60515. www.ivpress.com.

4. F. B. Meyers, *David* (Fort Washington, Penn.: Christian Literature Crusade, 1970). Used by permission.

5. Thomas Moore, *The Care of the Soul* (New York: HarperCollins, 1992), 166.

$\mathcal{N}otes$

Chapter 7

1. *Merriam-Webster's Collegiate Dictionary*, 10th ed., s.v. "hero."
2. Ernest Shackleton, *The Voyage of the Endurance* (New York: Carroll & Graf Publishers, 1998).
3. Gerhard Kittel, ed., and Geoffrey W. Bromiley, trans. and ed., *Theological Dictionary of the New Testament* (Grand Rapids, Mich.: Eerdmans, 1978), 1:507.
4. A. T. Robertson, *Word Pictures in the New Testament* (Nashville: Broadman and Holman, 2000), Luke 15:17.
5. Mary Bowley (Mrs. Peters), "Whom Have We, Lord, But Thee?" © 1856.
6. Samuel Davies, "Great God of Wonders," © 1769.

Chapter 8

1. Eugene Peterson, *Traveling Light* (Colorado Springs: Helmers and Howard, 1988), 67. Used by permission.
2. Brennan Manning, *Abba's Child* (Colorado Springs: NavPress, 1994), 79.
3. Burke Davis, *Marine! The Life of Chesty Puller* (New York: Random, 1991).
4. James Strong, *The Exhaustive Concordance of the Bible* (Nashville: Abingdon, 1973), G1111.
5. *Merriam-Webster's Collegiate Dictionary*, 10th ed., see "prodigal."
6. Gerhard Kittel, ed., and Geoffrey W. Bromiley, trans. and ed., *Theological Dictionary of the New Testament* (Grand Rapids, Mich.: Eerdmans, 1978), 1:507.
7. Henri J. M. Nouwen, *The Return of the Prodigal Son: A Story of Homecoming* (New York: Image Books, a division of Random House, 1994), 71.
8. Phillip Yancy, *What's So Amazing about Grace?* (Grand Rapids, Mich.: Zondervan, 1997), 11.

Chapter 9

1. Gary Bauer, *Our Journey Home* (Dallas: Word, 1992), 22–23.
2. "Grandpa (Tell Me 'Bout The Good Old Days)" © 1985 Sony/ATV Tunes LLC. All rights Adm. by Sony/ATV Music Publishing, 8 Music Sq. W., Nashville, TN 37203. All Rights Reserved. Used by permission.
3. Remarks of Mrs. Bush at Wellesley College Commencement, 1990. Used by permission.

Chapter 10

1. Brennan Manning, *Abba's Child* (Colorado Springs: NavPress, 1994), 72–73.
2. Taken from *Parents in Pain* by John White. Copyright © 1979 InterVarsity Christian Fellowship of the USA. Used with permission of InterVarsity Press, PO Box 1400, Downers Grove, IL 60515. www.ivpress.com.
3. R. Laird Harris, Gleason L. Archer, Jr., and Bruce K. Waltke, eds., *Theological Wordbook of the Old Testament*, Vol. (Chicago: Moody, 1999), 23.
4. Victor Harold Matthews, Mark W. Chavalas, and John H. Walton, *The IVP Bible Background Commentary: Old Testament* (Downers Grove, Ill.: InterVarsity Press, 200).

5. Thomas Moore, *The Care of the Soul* (New York: HarperCollins, 1992), 166.

6. Ann Ortlund, *Children Are Wet Cement* (Grand Rapids, Mich.: Fleming Revell, a division of Baker Books, 1981), 183–184.

Chapter 11

1. Michelle Schreder, *The Unexpected Gift* (Sisters, Ore.: VMI Publishers, 2004), 8.

2. Ibid., 118.

3. Joni Eareckson Tada and Steve Estes, *When God Weeps: Why Our Sufferings Matter to the Almighty* (Grand Rapids: Zondervan Publishing House, 1997), 83, 85–86.

Chapter 12

1. Winston Churchill, Grosvenor House, London, upon receiving "The Times" Literary Award, 2 November 1949.

2. Gilda Radner, *It's Always Something* (New York: Simon and Schuster, 2000), 237.

3. Gary Bauer, *Our Journey Home* (Dallas: Word, 1992), 132.

4. *Merriam-Webster's Collegiate Dictionary*, 10th ed., see "tolerance."

5. R. Laird Harris, Gleason L. Archer, Jr., and Bruce K. Waltke, eds., *Theological Wordbook of the Old Testament*, Vol. (Chicago: Moody, 1999), 802.

6. Reinhold Niebuhr, "Well-Intentioned Dragons," *Christianity Today*, 1985, 63.

About the Author

Dr. Charles R. Swindoll is senior pastor of Stonebriar Community Church, chancellor of Dallas Theological Seminary, and the Bible teacher on the internationally syndicated radio program *Insight for Living*. He has written more than thirty best-selling books, such as *Strengthening Your Grip*, *Laugh Again*, *The Grace Awakening*, and the million-selling Great Lives from God's Word series. Chuck and his wife, Cynthia, live in Frisco, Texas.

Ordinary People, Great Lives

ISBN 978-0-8499-1382-2 · ISBN 978-0-8499-1386-0 · ISBN 978-0-8499-1385-3 · ISBN 978-0-8499-1749-3

ISBN 978-0-8499-1383-9 · ISBN 978-0-8499-1342-6 · ISBN 978-0-8499-0016-7 · ISBN 978-0-8499-1389-1

The *Great Lives* series explores ordinary men and women whose lives were empowered by God when they surrendered to Him. Learn from the great lives of our faith and how their stories can help us become who we were created to be.

Through the *Great Lives* series, Dr. Swindoll explores the lives of biblical characters to find the qualities that made them great. Their lives show us what God considers to be great and that those characteristics lie within the reach of everyone who submits to Him.

Available Now

INSIGHT FOR LIVING

THOMAS NELSON
Since 1798

For other products and live events,
visit us at: thomasnelson.com

FEB 2012

CLIFTON PARK-HALFMOON PUBLIC LIBRARY, NY

0 00 06 03919184

CPSIA information can be obtained at www.ICGtesting.com
Printed in the USA
LVOW041109240112

265341LV00001B/16/P

9 781400 280032